The Ruins of Ani

The Ruins of Ani

Krikor Balakian

Translated and with an introduction by
Peter Balakian with Aram Arkun

RUTGERS UNIVERSITY PRESS
NEW BRUNSWICK, CAMDEN, AND NEWARK,
NEW JERSEY, AND LONDON

Library of Congress Cataloging-in-Publication
Control Number: 2018019235

A British Cataloging-in-Publication record for this book is available from
the British Library.

The Ruins of Ani was first published in Armenian by H. Matteosian Press
in Constantinople, 1910.
Translation and introduction to this edition copyright © 2019
by Peter Balakian

♾ The paper used in this publication meets the requirements of the
American National Standard for Information Sciences—Permanence of
Paper for Printed Library Materials, ANSI Z39.48-1992.

www.rutgersuniversitypress.org

Manufactured in the United States of America

To the memory of the Ani diggers:
Nicholas Marr, Toros Toromanian,
Hovsep Orbeli, Aram and Artashes Vruyr,
Arshak Fetvadjian, and the others.

Contents

Notes on the Translation

During the translation process of *Armenian Golgotha* (2009), my co-translator Aris Sevag came to some kind of insight about the spelling of Bishop Balakian's first name, which on the title page of *Armenian Golgotha* was Krikoris Balakian rather than Krikor, the name he used on his previous book *The Ruins of Ani*. In Armenian, these variations on names are used both formally and in the vernacular.

Sevag argued that when Krikor was ordained he would have taken the grabar (classical Armenian) spelling of his name as was the ritual, and thus his name would have been spelled Grigoris, rather than Krikoris. I deferred to Aris. In retrospect, I think, we should have left my great uncle's name as it was on the title page of the original edition of the book—Krikoris Balakian. Furthermore, Balakian wrote in Western Armenian and not Eastern Armenian, and so the *K* would have been appropriate.

Now faced with the issue of the spelling of his name on this earlier book, I have wrestled with keeping his name consistent—Grigoris—as it appeared on *Armenian Golgotha*, or being consistent with how his name appears on the title page of *The Ruins of Ani*. After consultation with my collaborator Aram Arkum and with Professor Christina Maranci, I have decided to be faithful to how his name appears on the title page. For readers, booksellers, and library catalogers, I hope that Krikor Balakian aka Grigoris Balakian will not present any problem in clarity.

* * *

Because Krikor Balakian wrote in Western Armenian, we are using Western Armenian for his text, but we are keeping classical Armenian for the medieval church wall inscriptions he quotes. Some spellings, such as the word Ararat, are rendered in their current popular spelling. I have used contemporary, Eastern Armenian spelling of certain proper nouns in my introduction. We have used Eastern Armenian with Western Armenian spelling in parentheses is in the glossary.

PB

Introduction

PETER BALAKIAN

The moment and context of the writing of *The Ruins of Ani* is one of historic drama embedded in a small, epic-like journey that the young *vartabed* (celibate priest), Krikor Balakian, made with twelve other clergymen in June 1909. The pilgrimage was led by Matteos II, the Catholicos of the Armenian Church, which defined the importance of the occasion. Balakian, who already had diplomatic responsibilities for the Armenian patriarchate in Constantinople (Istanbul), embarked on the pilgrimage with a passion to see this sacred place of which he had dreamed for so long. In 1909 the ruined medieval city of Ani was still part of the Russian Empire, and so the Catholicos, who was seated in the historic capital of the Armenian Church in Etchmiadzin, just 30 miles from Yerevan in Russian Armenia, was able to organize such a pilgrimage as part of a religious and cultural expedition.

At a certain moment near the end of this travel-memoir-history, Balakian confesses: "I was overjoyed at this opportunity to see Ani, I had a thirst to see those eternal monuments of the past glory of our forefathers. I wanted to kiss that holy soil." Balakian's affect is certainly not ambiguous; for him and, one might suggest, for the Armenian imaginary, Ani embodies a historical truth. This ruined medieval city was once a great capital city of "eternal monuments" and a center of Armenian civilization. For Balakian, then, the topography and landscape of the Shirak plain on which Ani is situated is a sacred geography. Arriving there in late June 1909, Balakian writes: "we could see the white-haired Masis [Mt. Ararat] proud and imperious, which as Khorenatsi wrote: 'sprouted like a tree from the earth.' The mountain rises like a colossal tree, or a monolithic tower of stone created by God . . . is not this mountain which rises on the heart of Armenia, a silent monument to the ancient glory and sorrow of the Armenians?" What could be more mythic to this priest: God, ancient glory, Mount Ararat, are all here as an original setting for Armenia's historical past.

The affective tone and the intellectual perspectives of *The Ruins of Ani* are often defined by discovery, astonishment, and, at times, even revelation. The reader of this compact, hybrid monograph will find that the energizing voice of the author (the young priest Krikor Balakian, who would later become the bishop of the Armenian Church of South France) creates a narrative that is both scholarly and personal.

To witness this excavation of Ani in June 1909 was to witness a kind of resurrection, a retrieval from the lost Armenian past—with the good news that, in some way Ani lives and that the Armenian past is still touchable, alive in some remnant way with implications. The news was: the Armenian past was glorious, and Armenians must, in whatever way, retrieve it. Nicholas Marr, the Russian archaeologist who began the great dig at Ani in 1892, exclaimed on this day [25] June 1909 to the Catholicos, Matteos, upon his arrival: "it's been almost nine centuries since a patriarchal visit to Ani has occurred." And, until now, Balakian informs us, "not one scientific investigation or excavation has been conducted, although various Armenian and European scholars have visited and studied Ani." There is, in Balakian's account of this pilgrimage, both a framing of the event and a framing of his monograph as historically significant.

The city of Ani occupied an area of about 200 acres on the Shirak plain in the Armenian Highlands in the southwest Caucasus, and today this area lies inside Turkey, abutting the border with the Armenian Republic. The city was founded by the Armenian

The main entrance gate and northern walls, constructed 989, renovations eleventh to thirteenth centuries.

Bagratuni (Pakraduni) Dynasty around 950 c.e. on what was then the famous Silk Road, and was the capital of the Armenian Kingdom. The citadel walls, still visible at the highest part of the ramparts, were built by the Armenian prince Ashot III in 960–61, and his grandson Smbat II built "the famous double ramparts to the north, nearly 3 miles long."[1] From its founding it became a place of obsessive church building, and so it accrued the name City of 1001 Churches, a symbolic phrase—but certainly there were scores of churches and chapels in the city and environs.

The Byzantines annexed the city in 1045. In 1064 Alp Arslan and the Seljuk Turks conquered Ani, and they installed the Kurdish Shaddadid emirs to rule the city until the Georgians conquered it in 1199. During this period both Armenian and Georgian princes known as the Zakarians ruled the city. The Mongols, during their imperial sweep into the Caucasus under Genghis Khan, conquered the city in 1239, and the legendary Tamerlane sacked the city in the 1380s. But upon his death the Turkish clans known as the Black Sheep (Kara Koyunlu) took over the city. A large earthquake destroyed much of the city during this period and sent the trade routes of that part of the Silk Road south to Anatolia and Mesopotamia. This added to the abandonment of the city by the fifteenth century, although Ani was part of the Safavid empire until it was taken by the Ottomans in 1579.[2] Although it remained a pilgrimage site and housed a monastery until the eighteenth century, Ani seems to have fallen out of all use. But in the early nineteenth century when European travelers returned from the region with reports about the ruins of Ani, new awareness of the history began to emerge.[3]

After the Russians annexed Ani and the Kars Oblast (province) following the Russo-Turkish war of 1877–78, there emerged a new interest in the site. By 1880 photographs of Ani by Ohannes Kurkdjian were being sold in stereoscopic sets. And in the next decade, the Imperial Academy of Sciences in St. Petersburg sponsored the first excavation project, which was conducted by Nicholas Marr, an "Orientalist" of the Caucasus who was also a linguist, historian, and budding archaeologist when in 1892 he began his first dig at Ani. Marr, who was trained at St. Petersburg University and would later become a faculty member there, conducted a dig and a scholarly recovery project, which led to his founding the Ani museum on the grounds. Marr's work was supported by Russian and Armenian scholars and benefactors, and his team surveyed and mapped the site, excavated and restored various buildings, collected significant artifacts, and published scientific studies in journals giving rise to a modern discourse about the city and its history. Among the Armenian collaborators were the architect and historian Toros Toramanian; the medievalist Hovsep Orbeli, who later became the director of the Hermitage Museum; the photographers Aram Vruyr and his son Artashes; and the painter Arshak Fetvadjian, who created a visual record of the site and its evolving form.[4]

During the period from 1892 to 1915 Ani was, for Armenians, a symbol of lost glory and political power and autonomy as well as an emblem of cultural pride and hope for a new future. During

World War I, in which the Armenian Genocide was carried out, Marr's work was halted and then assaulted as war broke out between the Russian and the Ottoman armies. When the Russian army left the war in 1917 in the wake of the Bolshevik Revolution and victory, Turkey took control of Ani and the Kars province. Then, in the war between the newly hatched Republic of Armenia and Turkey in 1918, the Armenian army, comprising genocide refugees and survivors, managed to take control of Kars province for a short time before it lost it again to the Turks in 1920. The expedient Treaty of Kars in 1922 made between the new Soviet Union and the Turkish government wrestled Kars, and Ani with it, away from Armenia. In a strange occurrence in the spring of 1921, the commander of the Third Ottoman army, Kazim Karabekir was ordered by Ataturk to destroy "every single stone of these Ani ruins, and to abolish their trace from the face of the earth."[5] And, for whatever reasons, Karabekir did not follow through with the order. Some of Ani was ransacked and destroyed and some of it left as it was, and as Christina Miranci notes, the museum on site was destroyed: "its doors pried off the hinges and the roofs removed"; in some accounts the artifacts were sent by train to Tiflis and disappeared and in other accounts the contents of the museum were buried in various locations.[6]

Among other things, *The Ruins of Ani* affords a kind of topological view of Ani from an early twentieth-century Armenian intellectual perspective. The idea of Ani as a site of Armenian historical achievement and a place of historical memory had been a current in Armenian contemporary culture since the 1890s when Nicholas Marr began his excavations of the city. Balakian quotes Catholicos Matteos II speaking at the public moment of reception to Professor Marr at the gates of Ani in late June of 1909: "Through your excavations, you reveal to the whole world the true picture of the magnificent past of a misfortunate and exiled people." The Catholicos's words here bring the past and present into a dialectical awareness that defines "this Ani moment" in which past glory and present suffering are part of a conjoined history.

The grounds of Ani, May 2015.

Balakian's own take on this dialectic of the past and present in the Armenian predicament is embedded in his use of Dante in his introduction: "What is more grievous and heartrending than to recall the glory of past days when one is living in days of misfortune." Balakian's take on Dante bears an affirmative twist: "it is not *only* grievous," he continues, "but it is on the contrary, consoling." And, the consolation is that it reminds us of a grand Armenian past: "Armenian glory," "Armenian genius," "the living," and "eternal monuments" that are Ani. For Balakian, this is inspiring, an emblem of hope and possible cultural revitalization.

The Ruins of Ani is also an investigation of the architectural and aesthetic achievements of tenth-century Armenian architecture. Using the work of H.F.B. Lynch and Charles Texier, Balakian argues that what Lynch called "Armenia's native genius," and singular talent . . . in the art and technology of architecture" were a

Broken stone bridge over the Akhurian River, circa tenth to thirteenth centuries.

foundation for medieval European Gothic architecture and deserve their rightful place in history:

> While Lynch ascribes the origin of Gothic architecture to the East, another scholar, the Frenchman [Charles] Texier goes a step further with a definite assertion that the Gothic style has an Armenian origin, and that the architectural chef d'oeuvre style, Gothic, had come to central Europe by means of emigration from the city of Arpa Chay, which is another name for Ani and the Turkish name of the Akhurian River.
>
> Thus, when the first invasions of Ani by Alp Arslan began in 1064, some of the population began to migrate in groups to Poland, Wallachia, Moldavia, and central Europe, and they brought with them, among other things, their arts and crafts. Thus the Armenians of Ani created a foundation in medieval central Europe for the incomparable Gothic style, which in its forms and variety of

Akhurian River snaking along the eastern border (closed by the Turkish government) of Ani between Turkey and Armenia.

beautiful carving and stonework was the chef d'oeuvre of all architectural styles.

I would note among those monumental achievements of Gothic architecture: Venice's San Marco basilica, Milan's cathedral, Paris's Notre Dame, and London's Westminster Abbey, each known

Main cathedral built by the architect Trdat circa 950–1000. (Courtesy of Christina Maranci.)

to the world as glorious expressions of Gothic architecture from their respective historical moments. Thus, Ani's renowned cathedral bears the early imprint of Gothic architecture. Its tall and delicate columns, its ovoid interior, and its hollow arches have inspired marvel in European scholarly travelers.

Balakian's observations of the achievements of Armenian medieval church architecture are perceptive, and anyone who visits an Armenian medieval church today will probably corroborate what he notes:

If we wish to summarize the chief characteristics of the Armenian architectural style of the buildings of Ani, we can say the following: (1) General simplicity of the style of the architectural plan; (2) Integrity, and in various parts perfect harmony of the architectural structure; (3) In order to avoid monotony, abundance of arches, pillars, and carvings and particular regularity in ornamentation, without

boastful superfluity; (4) Decorum and rich variety of carved ornamentation; (5) A mysterious darkness that is observable in this type
of ancient Armenian construction, which is neither darkness nor
light, and which leaves the viewer with a mystical feeling or experience. This corresponds with the church's aim of nourishing the
soul; (6) The pointed cupola positioned in the middle of Armenian
temples is also a native characteristic of Armenian architecture; no
other Christian church has this feature, and we find it, beginning
with the cathedral of Holy Etchmiadzin, on the majority of old
and new Armenian churches in the Caucasus.

For Balakian, Trdat was the innovative architect of the era—a
canonical figure for Armenians, and the man who designed the Ani
Cathedral with groundbreaking techniques. He was so respected
that he was called to Constantinople in 990 by the Byzantine
emperor Basil II to renovate Hagia Sophia after an earthquake dev-
astated the church. Although Balakian celebrates the achievement
of other churches at Ani, such as Tigran Honents/St. Gregory
(Krikor) the Illuminator, the Church of the Holy Savior, and the
Church of the Holy Apostles, he dwells on the Cathedral as the
jewel in the crown. For him, Trdat's masterpiece is the monument
"full of grace," and "of the highest artistic merit, denoting a standard of culture which was far in advance of the contemporary
standards in the West." Here, as in his reflection on other moments
at Ani, Balakian's exuberance veers toward a tone of romantic
Armenian exceptionalism, but he does, of course, note the impact of
Arabic, Byzantine, and Persian traditions on Armenian building.

He introduces the reader to features of the Armenian decorative
and aesthetic traditions—their brilliance and beauty; he underscores the art of the masonry, both interior and exterior, and the
carefully polished tufa stones of the churches which are exemplary
artistic manifestations of the Shirak region. Balakian points out that
"the [stones] are joined with such refinement," and this has "been a
subject of amazement for scholarly visitors." The "creative and aesthetic skill" of this masonry also comes from an understanding and
use of the range of the stone's color: tan, brown, chocolate, red, pink,
gray. He also notes that the elaborate inscriptions (the epigraphs)

on exterior walls are decoratively elegant and intellectually rich, and each "sheds light on . . . Armenian civilization, and on the character, and moral and intellectual state of the Armenian people at that time."

"A misfortunate and exiled people"—let me return to those words of the Catholicos in his public speech that day with Nicholas Marr in June 1909. The words open into the other dominant narrative of *The Ruins of Ani*—one that is both historical and contemporary.

There is a dialectic running through the narrative in which Armenian exceptionalism—the once triumphant civilization embodied by Ani—is contrasted with a history of conquest, colonization, and ruin—often a conquest at the hands of Turkic tribes—Sultan Alp Arslan and the Seljuks, Genghis Khan, Ogedei Khan and Charmaghan, and Tamerlane. The historical narrative of Armenia has been defined by periods of autonomy and peace and then conquest, ruin, and persecution. The invasion of Ani by Seljuk Turk warrior Alp Arslan in 1064 begins an evolving typology of conquest and destruction that defines most of the remaining history of Ani. Balakian exclaims that "Ani speaks more to the heart of the Armenian visitor than to the eye, for these ruins still bear the imprint of the vandalism and barbarism of the Arabs, Seljuks, Persians, and Greeks." He continually refers to those "greedy enemies" who pillaged and conquered "this magnificent capital of the Pakraduni Kings."

He also reminds us that "the pages of Armenian history do not bear a blacker and more fiendish inscription than of the expeditions of Genghis Khan's Tatars. And Genghis Khan's successor (Ogedei Khan)'s large army under the commander Charmaghan would conquer and pillage Ani as well, as would Byzantines, Georgians, Kurds, and Mongols. And in 1387 Tamerlane, seeking to restore Genghis Khan's power, destroyed Ani so thoroughly that it "became uninhabited," ending the presence of Armenia's royal capital.

But the history of conquest and ruin is inseparable from the present. In this moment of June 1909 and the ensuing year when Balakian was writing this monograph, the condition of the Armenians

Church of St. Krikor (Abughamrents). (Courtesy of Christina Maranci.)

in the Ottoman Empire was sliding backward. In the southern region of Adana in April 1909 a horrendous episode of massacre exploded. The new Young Turk regime had come to power in 1908 after a nonviolent revolution, conducted by the military, had deposed Sultan Abdul Hamid II from his political control of the empire (he would remain caliph of all Sunni Muslims of the empire). The revolution promised constitutional changes for Christian and other minorities in what was hoped to be a new, more democratic system. The progressive, new regime introduced some constitutional changes aimed at inclusion of ethnic minorities, but the changes were never enacted, in part, because the flow of reactionary backlash from conservative Islamic factions and loyalists to the sultan led to a counterrevolution in the spring of 1909. And the bloodiest episodes of this counterrevolution were carried out against the Armenian population in the city and environs of Adana. In a region where there was even more poverty and political corruption than the sagging empire was hampered by, Armenians were a target for the intense backlash against Christian minorities. Armenians and Greeks were economically well off in Adana, and this too spurred resentment. The counterrevolution led to the looting of Armenian businesses in the city, which set off a month of mass killing of Armenians in what one historian called the "worst blood bath in modern history."[7] In the end, between 20,000 and 30,000 were dead.

What had preceded the Adana massacres less than twenty years earlier had been an even more extreme episode of mass violence. The massacres in the Abdul Hamid period erupted in 1894 in retaliation to Armenian protests for tax reform and other peaceful, civic protests for constitutional protections of minorities. Over a two-year period (1894–96) between 100,000 and 200,000 Armenian civilians were killed—only for their ethnic identity. It was a campaign of unprecedented mass violence in modern history, and it elicited relief and rescue efforts from across Europe and the United States that were also unprecedented. Thus the elation among Armenians during the period of Ani's uncovering arose in a context fraught with the reign of terror and massacre. And this complex situation helps us to understand this moment in Vartabed Balakian's historiographical view. Reading *The Ruins of Ani* in the wake of the Adana massacres, one might see this monograph as a reclamation of historic Armenia with its hope for a cultural renaissance in the coming age.

The Armenian Genocide and Cultural Destruction

Within five years of the publication of *The Ruins of Ani*, Krikor Balakian would be among the 250 cultural leaders arrested in Constantinople on April 24, 1915. And after surviving nearly four years in prisons and camps and in wilderness, disguised as a German soldier, Greek vineyard worker, German engineer, among other guises, he wrote his memoir of his four years in the killing fields, *Armenian Golgotha*.[8] His survivor memoir remains today a key text in the witness memory of the Genocide. And looking back, one can see too that *The Ruins of Ani* reverberates in another pertinent way because it affords us a view of the significance of cultural property and its destruction as a component of genocide.

The eradication of the Armenian population in Turkey in 1915 has been noted as the first episode of genocide carried out in a modern form, which is to distinguish it from genocide carried out in premodern modes, often in the contexts of conquest, colonialism, and war starting in antiquity and continuing into the early twentieth century with the destruction of the Herero of Namibia by the Germans.[9] However, unlike genocidal campaigns before 1915, the Ottoman Turkish extermination of the Armenians is marked by certain salient features that define what came to be modern genocide: the focused use of government apparatus—bureaucracy, military, technology and communications, and nationalist ideology—in order to first target and isolate and then eliminate an ethnic or cultural group—that is, a stateless subgroup of the larger population—in a concentrated period of time.

Looking back at the twentieth century, one can see that the Armenian Genocide was a seminal event in the evolution of what genocide in the modern era would become. When Adolph Hitler said to his military advisers, eight days before invading Poland in 1939, "Who, today, after all, speaks of the annihilation of the Armenians?"[10] he was using the example of the success of the Ottoman government's ruling party in 1915 (Committee of Union and Progress, hereafter, CUP), in eliminating a targeted minority population from Turkey. And he was emboldened by the fact that what had been in Europe and North America a highly publicized human rights disaster had disappeared from popular consciousness less than two decades later.

In conceptualizing the Armenian Genocide, it is important to note the significance of cultural destruction as a crucial dimension of the Ottoman government's final solution for the Armenians. The burning and razing of churches; the torture of men, women, and children with Christian crosses; the mass killing of Armenian intellectuals; and the forced conversion of Armenians to Islam were continual acts of assault from the 1894 to 1896 period of the Hamidian massacres to the 1909 Adana massacres and on through the period of genocide from 1915 until the end of World War I. These modes of violence embody the destruction of culture that Raphael Lemkin—who formulated the concept of genocide as a human rights crime—conceived of as part of the act. Lemkin understood genocide as involving both the mass killing of people in a targeted ethnic group and the destruction of their culture.[11]

What we see in the Armenian Genocide is a range of the decimation of culture. In conjunction with the mass killing and forced marches of the Armenian population, the Ottoman bureaucracy was focused on destroying, silencing, or appropriating (1) cultural property, (2) cultural producers: intellectuals, artists, teachers, clergy, (3) institutions that bear belief–value systems, and (4) historical territory—its cultural identity and significance.[12] The Armenian patriarch Malachia Ormanian compiled statistics in 1912–13 at the request of the Ottoman government. The statistics showed that there were 2,538 Armenian churches; during the Genocide all except a handful were plundered, taken over, set on fire, razed or demolished.[13] Similarly the 1912–13 census also shows that there were at least 1,996 Armenian schools and 451 Armenian monasteries, almost all of which were destroyed.[14] These facts are pertinent to the issues surrounding the ruins of Ani today, for the CUP's destruction of Armenian churches and schools was inseparable from the project of eradicating Armenian identity and history throughout Turkey, significant portions of which were historic Armenia.

One deep-seated fear among the Ottoman ruling elite was the historical legitimacy of Armenian civilization on its indigenous lands in much of central and eastern Turkey. Along with the Greeks, Assyrians, and Kurds, the Armenians were a salient, indigenous civilization of Anatolia, which had come under Ottoman rule by the sixteenth century. Armenians were natives going back to about the sixth century B.C.E. and had flourished as an empire across Anatolia and the Armenian Highlands during the reign of Tigran the Great in the first century B.C.E. They had also established a significant kingdom in southern Anatolia during the Middle Ages, known as Lesser or Cilician Armenia. For about 2,500 years then, Armenians had maintained a continuous culture in significant parts of the territory that would become Ottoman Turkey. They were a distinctive ethnic group, culturally and intellectually defined, by their becoming the first nation to declare Christianity its religion in 301.[15] And much of the evidence of Armenia's historical continuity was embedded in the churches, monasteries, and schools and in various forms of public and sacred art, including the omnipresent *khatchkars* (large carved stone crosses) that were found in cemeteries, churches, and other civic spaces in all Armenian towns and sections of cities. Not only were the churches destroyed by the gendarmes, killing squads, and local populations but many of the more than 2,500 churches were subsequently turned into barns, arsenals, brothels, artillery training areas, restaurants, night clubs, and cafes. And in the case of the ruined churches of Ani, the remaining buildings and ruins have been deliberately misnamed as Hittite or Byzantine in the site signage and in the tourist guides and maps in order to cover up their Armenian identity. The Armenian writing inside the churches has been painted out.[16]

Post-Genocide Legacy

The legacy of cultural destruction in any genocidal history plays out in complex ways. The Armenian aftermath is inseparable from the predicament of both exile and exclusion from its own historical past. Many of the ruins of Armenian monuments and buildings, sacred and secular, have been demolished, appropriated, and eroded by negligence and assault since 1915. The landscape of Turkey is covered with ruins of Armenian churches among other architectural monuments. And even the remains have been subject to continued erosion and removal throughout Turkey over the past decades.

Because of Turkey's state policy of denial of the Armenian Genocide history and its unwillingness to make any gestures of apology or restitution, or even to show minimal concern for the victimized culture, and because of the history of oppression of minorities in Turkey from the birth of the modern Turkish republic in 1923 through the present, the land and places of most of historic Armenia inside Turkey, have been walled off to Armenians both inside and outside of Turkey. The 60,000 Armenians living in Turkey today have access to the patriarchate and several other churches in Istanbul, but the rest of Turkey is, for them, no different than for the Armenians in the Republic and Diaspora.

Although Armenian tourists can view some of these sites for brief moments on tourist-controlled visits, they can do so only in a context defined by police surveillance and a state tourist industry that mislabels the ruins and structures in order to deny Armenian historical identity, and the ruins come to haunt the Armenian communities in ongoing ways. Inside the Turkish state, Armenian ruins are taboo and represent a forbidden past, an irreclaimable history, a paradox of an embodied absence, one in which loss and the widening exilic gap amplify each other. Looking on from the Armenian–Turkish border, at the ruins of Ani, into a zone that is closed by Turkey with barbed wire and military guards, adds another dimension to the aftermath of what I call the Armenian lockout-predicament.

Whether an Armenian is looking on from the Republic of Armenia that borders northeastern Turkey, or from the Middle East, Europe, North and South America, Russia, Australia, or elsewhere, in the Armenian diasporic experience, the ruins of material culture are forbidden, locked away, boarded up. And this predicament creates another dimension of trauma. Not only does the "exilic gap," as

Signage, City of Ani, no mention of Armenia.

Hamid Naficy calls it, "never close"[17] but in the Armenian case, I would suggest, the sense of loss grows within witnessing of continual ruin.

Furthermore, in the age of Internet gazing, instant image-news on the Internet, zeroing in on terrains and places with Google Earth, Armenians, like other diasporan cultures, can watch their monuments erode and disappear in unprecedented ways. The recent episode of a fashion shoot by Turkey's *Elle Magazine* at Ani, in the fall of 2011, brought the complexity of virtual reality, capitalism, commodification, and cultural property into a kind of semiotic performance.[18] As Turkish fashion models were depicted in alluring poses for advertising high fashion and sexy clothes amid and inside the ruins of the churches of Ani, Armenians around the world expressed their anger and shock. Thus, the materiality of the monuments can become a paradoxical absence–presence that reifies the wound. The Armenian gaze on these sites is, in some way, inextricable from the event of the Genocide and the continuous denial by successive Turkish governments. The taboo and falsified status of vanishing Armenian ruins inside Turkey remain a material emblem of an unresolved, traumatic history.

One recent manifestation of the continued trauma of the Armenian post-genocide predicament is dramatized in a congressional resolution proposed by the Armenian, Greek, and Assyrian communities in the United States in June 2011. House Resolution 306 "Urging the Republic of Turkey to safeguard its Christian heritage and to return confiscated church properties" to the Armenian, Assyrian, and Greek communities whose cultural heritages were destroyed by the Ottoman Empire in 1915. It was passed by the U.S. House Committee on Foreign Relations by a vote of 43–1 on July 21, 2011.

The resolution embodies in its scope and focus on the loss of its material culture and ensuing cultural remains in Turkey, a creative attempt to deal with the lockout predicament. Arguing that Turkey as signatory of the Universal Declaration of Human Rights has affirmed the freedom of religious belief and the practice of religious worship, and that Turkey has been cited now three years in a row by the United States Commission on International Religious Freedom for imposing "serious limitations on freedom of religion or belief," the Armenian community in the United States asks Turkey to allow free religious practice and

> (3) the return to their rightful owners all Christian churches and other places of worship, monasteries, schools, hospitals, monuments, relics, holy sites, and other religious properties, including movable properties, such as artwork, manuscripts, vestments, vessels, and other artifacts; and
>
> (4) all the rightful Christian church and lay owners of Christian church properties, without hindrance or restriction, to preserve, reconstruct, and repair, as they see fit, all Christian churches and other places of worship, monasteries, school, hospitals, monuments, relics, holy sites, and other religious properties within Turkey.[19]

The language of H. Res. 306 underscores a dimension of a protracted trauma and a need to reestablish a socially viable and active relationship with cultural identity and historical tradition and place, in order to make a bridge across the big hiatus of the post-genocide predicament.

Current Situation

In the past decade there has been a collaborative effort to save and restore Ani. In 1996 the World Monuments Fund designated two major Armenian Churches—the main Cathedral and the Church of the Holy Savior—as endangered world monuments and put them on their Watch Program. Since that moment of international recognition, the WMF has undertaken a "documentation and conservation program that has resulted in the stabilization of the two churches and in improvements in the larger landscape of the city."[20] Subsequently, the WMF's work brought in support from the Norwegian Institute for Cultural Heritage, and this has led to degrees of collaboration with the Turkish Ministry of Culture and Tourism, and two Turkish nongovernmental organizations, Osman Kavala's Anadolu Kültür, and the Research Center for Anatolian Civilizations at Koç University. Since 2006, new collaborations between the Turkish Ministry of Culture and Tourism and the WMF, together with an international group of scholars and professional experts, have brought greater international awareness about Ani, as well as higher preservation standards, including careful documentation and more transparent methods of restoration.

In the fall of 2013 these organizations sponsored a weeklong workshop at Ani during which an international group of scholars, including Turks and Armenians, met to assess the current state of the major and endangered buildings at Ani and in the surrounding region. The group established what they called a Risk Assessment Matrix in which they ranked 28 structures for their significance and for their vulnerability on scales of 1 to 25 and 1 to 35, respectively. They used the following rubrics to help formulate their assessments: (1) heritage significance, (2) intactness of building form, (3) exterior significant fabric, (4) interior significant fabric, (5) archaeological remains.[21] The impressive publication *Ani in Context* (2014) represents a step forward in the process of recovery and restoration and in various ways is in conversation with Balakian's *The Ruins of Ani*.

Nevertheless, restoration has started and stopped over the past decade because politics and logistical challenges have interceded. The restorations of various sites, including the Armenian churches of Tigran Honents (St. Gregory the Illuminator), Holy Savior, and the Main cathedral, are on hold at the moment, and the only ongoing work on the site is related to the Surp Prkitch (Holy Savior) church. This project has been overseen by the Turkish architect Yavuz Özkaya within the frame of an agreement between the Ministry of Culture and the WMF, which is using funds from the U.S. Ambassadors Fund. Armen Kazaryan, an Armenian scholar of architectural history, who teaches in Moscow, is also an adviser, and this creates some small spirit of Armenian–Turkish collaboration. Yavuz has also made an agreement with an Armenian architect and masonry expert who has cut stones in Armenia and brought them to Ani to install on the walls.

There is a similar cooperation agreement between the Ministry and the WMF regarding the Cathedral. However, this is still in a planning phase, and no work has been done on the site. Similarly, there have been excavations around the Cathedral and Surp Prkitch in order to create better access to the foundations and to unearth the stones that have fallen from the structures. Earlier, the Menuchir mosque and the Tigran Honents church had some restoration to shore them up. And the erosion of the buildings of Ani that has occurred since Balakian took his extraordinary photographs in 1909, which are included in this edition, is alarming.

The inclusion of Ani in UNESCO's list of World Heritage Sites has given some impetus and stature to the restoration project. And tourism has also been an impetus for Turkey to move ahead because the region is poor and whatever economy it would generate would be welcome. Turkey's nomination of Ani to UNESCO's Heritage List also has a pragmatic dimension because it improves Turkey's international image. Although the Turkish government has found it convenient to claim that these gestures toward collaboration

Church of Tigran Honents, close view.

indicate some genuine concern for Armenian heritage in Turkey, this is still window dressing. The fundamental problem remains: the Turkish government has not engaged in historically truthful restoration of the buildings of Ani nor in any accountability for the history of the human rights crimes committed against the Armenians, Greeks, and Assyrians in the first decades of the twentieth century, and this includes the massive range of destruction of Armenian heritage and culture throughout Turkey.

Turkey appears far from dealing with these ethical realities, and in its proposal to UNESCO, even the use of the word *Armenia* is remarkably rare. The official narrative emphasizes the multicultural characteristics of Ani with pagan, Christian, and Muslim monuments and the presence of Seljuk, Armenian, and Georgian architectural traditions. And now, with the new ultra–right wing government of President Erdogan what can we expect in the future?

In the fall of 2016 noted philanthropist and businessman Osman Kavala, art historian Christina Maranci, Ottoman historian Rachel Goshgarian, and I met at the United Nations with the

Interior of the main cathedral, whitewashed apse in background.

United Nations Development Programme (UNDP) (Ms. Cihan Sultanoglu, the director of the Regional Bureau for Europe and the Commonwealth of Independent States) and WMF. In that meeting there was a strong feeling that the designation of Ani in 2016 as a UNESCO World Heritage Site would help to safeguard the site and further efforts to stabilize the monuments. However, our meeting did not result in the Turkish government bringing the UNDP aboard. In 2016, Mr. Kavala was planning to prepare an exhibition on Ani, which he hoped would bring more attention to the project, and he announced that "the objective of his proposed exhibit would be to expose the masterpieces and the landscape with strong visual material, and to try to find a language which should describe the Armenianness of Ani as well as the multicultural richness of the city." Kavala had previously brought together the Turkish architect Yavuz with two Turkish and Armenian photographers and the scholar Armen Kazaryan. But then politics intervened, and in the current reign of terror and purges that President Erodgan is conducting in the wake of the failed coup of July 2016, the chances for any movement on restoration at Ani and historical truth reckoning seem slim. And then, in October 2017, Mr. Kavala—one of the most prominent, humane, and generous philanthropists and forces for democracy in Turkey—was arrested and imprisoned on fabricated charges that he was conspiring to overthrow the Turkish state. The international outcry for his release is another expression of moral protest against the evaporation of intellectual freedom in Turkey today.

But, the question remains: can the restoration of Ani become a bridge between the Republic of Armenia and Turkey today? In the wake of the Armenian Genocide and in the matrix of the Turkish state's denial of its crimes against the Armenian people and their culture, history, and heritage, can there be a fully realized effort to recover Ani? The idea of recovery is essential because it is predicated on the idea that restoration must entail an honest and truthful representation of the historical facts of the city—its origins and its cultural achievements.

As one can see from the current signage at Ani, placed by the Turkish Board of Tourism in the past decade, there has been no progress on this front. Even though the older blue signs were replaced with the more modern white and black signs about a decade ago, there is still no mention of the word *Armenia* on any them, although there are a few names of Armenian historical figures like the architect Trdat and the Bagratuni dynasty, but without context or identification of their Armenian identities. Even the name of the city has been changed in the official Turkish documentation: instead of Ani (Arm. Անի), it has become Anı, which translates in Turkish as "memory"—the irony of which has not gone unnoticed by scholars and commentators.[22] The situation remains: at the site of Armenia's most important medieval city there is no official designation of the city's Armenian history and buildings. Tourists and visitors Turkish and non-Turkish would have to recognize on their own that the dramatic inscriptions carved into the stone exteriors of some of the churches are medieval Armenian inscriptions. Or the tourist who is intrigued by the word *Bagratuni* might do

Church of the Holy Redeemer, undergoing restoration by the World Monuments Fund.

a quick search on her iPhone to find that the word refers to the Armenian rulers of the region in the tenth century. Ani does bear the layers of its history and it also has buildings from the Seljuk, Georgian, Mongol, and Byzantine conquests and periods of rule. But Ani was founded and built by a great Armenian dynastic family and remains a central place in Armenian history.

In addition to its intellectual and historical contributions, *The Ruins of Ani* offers another building block to an imagined bridge between Turkey and the Armenian Republic and Diaspora. Balakian's monograph contributes the historical truth and cultural evidence that are necessary in creating a responsible dialogue between the two cultures. Ani could become a heritage site of hope and of peace, a place of cultural and political negotiation in the wake of the post-Genocide impasse between Turkey and the Armenians. It is a unique site that has the potential to open a space between the two cultures. One can see in Ani a place and opportunity in which

Signage, City of Ani, no mention of Armenia.

the Armenian Republic and Armenian Diaspora and Turkey might negotiate a way toward truth and reconciliation. The ethical issues that emerge from the gridlock of Turkish denialism and the Armenian quest for social justice are dramatic. Armenia's most important, intact ruin lies inside Turkey, wedged at the Armenian–Turkish border; its presence haunts the Republic of Armenia and the Armenian Diaspora. Ani's falsified reality represents one more self-destructive and dysfunctional manifestation of Turkish nationalism. It was not a coincidence that the *New York Times* put a large color photograph of the ruins of Ani as the lead image on the front page (April 17, 2015) for its story on the one hundredth anniversary of the Armenian Genocide. The headline read: "A Century After a Genocide Turkey's Denial Only Deepens." The image of Ani still haunts us today and remains an emblem of the failed reckoning on the part of Turkey.

Ani is, today, a popular tourist site for anyone traveling to the region, but its revenues belong to Turkey, and the irony is not lost

Tigran Honents church sign, the word Armenian absent.

on anyone. Given the massive destruction of Armenian lives and Armenian property conducted by the Ottoman Turkish empire and modern Turkish state in the past hundred and thirty years, it would be a small gesture of social justice for Turkey to return Ani to the Armenian Republic, which abuts Ani at its western border.

Many options could ensue and Armenia and Turkey could share tourist revenue and restoration priorities and practices. Might the lost city not become an example to the world about how cultural heritage can play an ethical role in conflict resolution? If Turkey were able to acknowledge the Armenian historical past, it would be an organic gesture forward, one that would help both Turkey and Armenia.

Ani offers the possibility of becoming a mutually beneficial, historical site—and a place of meeting where truth must precede reconciliation. The banishment of the word *Armenia* at Ani continues to create a sense of the absurd, and this serves both Turkey and Armenia badly. The call for a continued and robust restoration project at Ani offers an unusual geopolitical opportunity. Notwithstanding Turkey's current tenor of state repression and extreme nationalism, there will be a future with new directions. And Ani can embody one of them. The still sizeable remains of this historic Armenian city should not have to wait much longer for its truth.

Notes

Photos in the Introduction are by Peter Balakian unless noted otherwise.

1. Heghnar Zeitlian Watenpaugh, "Preserving the Medieval City of Ani: Cultural Heritage between Contest and Reconciliation," *Journal of the Society of Architectural Historians* 73, no. 4 (December 2014): 531.

2. Maranci, Christina, *The Art of Armenia: An Introduction* (New York: Oxford University Press, 2018), 270.

3. Watenpaugh, 531–532.

4. Ibid., 532–533.

5. Vahakn N. Dadrian, "The Role of Turkish Physicians in the World War I Genocide of Ottoman Armenians," *Holocaust and Genocide Studies* 1, no. 2 (1986): 169–192.

6. Christina Marinci, "Krikor Balakian's *The Ruins of Ani*: A Surprising Source for Armenian Architecture," *Venezia Arti* (Ca' Foscari), special volume, *Historiography of the South Caucasus,* ed. Ivan Foletti (December 2018).

7. Vahakn N. Dadrian, *The History of the Armenian Genocide: Ethnic Conflict from the Balkans to Anatolia to the Caucasus* (New York: Berghahn Books, 2003), 183.

8. Grigoris Balakian, *Armenian Golgotha*, trans. Peter Balakian with Aris Sevag. (New York: Alfred A. Knopf, 2009), chap. 6, 7.

9. Peter Balakian, "The Armenian Genocide and the Modern Age," *The Sydney Papers* 20, no. 2 (Autumn 2008): 145–160.

10. Louis P. Lochner, *What about Germany?* (New York: Dodd, Mead, & Co., 1942), 2.

11. Raphael Lemkin, "Genocide as a Crime under International Law," Raphael Lemkin Collection, Manuscript Collection P-154, American Jewish Historical Society at the Center for Jewish History, New York City, New York (hereafter AJHS), Box 6, Folder 2, undated, p. 2. Available online at http://digital.cjh.

12. Peter Balakian, "Raphael Lemkin, Cultural Destruction, and the Armenian Genocide," *Journal of Holocaust Studies* 27, no.1 (Spring 2013): 63–64.

13. Ara Sarafian, ed., *U.S. Official Documents of the Armenian Genocide*, vol. 2, *The Peripheries* (Watertown, M.A.: Armenian Review Press, 1994), xiv, xvi.

14. Sarafian, *U.S. Official Documents of the Armenian Genocide*, xvi.

15. Peter Balakian, *The Burning Tigris: The Armenian Genocide and America's Response*, (New York: HarperCollins, 2003), 29–33.

16. Simon Maghakyan, "Cultural Genocide: Photo-Documents on the Destruction of the Armenian Heritage in Turkey," 2005, DVD.

17. Hamid Naficy, *An Accented Cinema: Exilic and Diasporic Filmmaking* (Princeton, NJ: Princeton University Press, 2001), 164.

18. Balakian, "Raphael Lemkin, Cultural Destruction, and the Armenian Genocide," 83.

19. H. Res. 306, "Urging the Republic of Turkey to safeguard its Christian heritage and to return confiscated properties." 112th Congress of the United States, 1st Session.

20. *Ani in Context Workshop*, New York (New York: World Monuments Fund, 2014), 6.

21. Ibid., 7.

22. Maranci, *The Art of Armenia: an Introduction*, 272; Watenpaugh, "Preserving the Medieval City of Ani," 545.

The Ruins of Ani

Very Rev. Fr. Krikor Balakian
Description of Ani's Ruins:
Illustrated

———

A. History
B. Topography
C. Description
D. Scholarship

CONSTANTINOPLE
H. MATTEOSIAN PRESS
1910

Dedicated to His Holiness Patriarch Matteos II
the Most Holy Catholicos of All Armenians
of the Mother See of Ararat with Filial Gratitude

Preface

Although Ani is close to the heart of every deep-feeling Armenian, it is equally unknown to the Armenian people. Armenians know very little about this museum of national antiquity, which is also a living witness to the ancient glory of Armenian civilization.

Although European and occasionally some Armenian critics are critical of, or even try to refute, some of the work of the classical Armenian historians by claiming that Khorenatsi's writings about the origins of the Armenians are fables, nobody can refute the nearly five centuries of history of the Pakraduni [Bagratid] era.[1] This is not only because the Pakraduni period is closer to us, but also because the royal era of the Pakradunis is also defined by its famous capital of *Ani*. Among its ruins, the archaeologist or scholar will find abundant material for a study of the historical state of Armenian civilization from the ninth to thirteenth centuries. And for the most part, Armenian historians have passed over these centuries so superficially and have only paid close attention to the foreign and domestic wars with which Armenians were involved.

Indeed, whoever wants to know about the Armenians must go to Ani. There he can learn many things, and study this period of

---

1. The transcription system used here reflects the Modern Western Armenian usage; commonly known historical names of persons and places are given in classical transcription in the church wall texts that are quoted and are in brackets in the general text.

Armenian civilization. And there is a great deal at Ani for the archaeologist and scholar to observe and assess. Even in its sad state, Ani conveys many things to the inquisitive visitor. Even if a visitor's first impression is one of sadness at Ani's state of ruin, a scrutinizing eye will see what an extraordinary level Armenian civilization had reached in the Middle Ages, especially in comparison with its neighbors.

Although serious studies about Ani have been published, among which illustrated ones are not lacking, they have been written mostly by European travelers and published in foreign languages [non Armenian, tr.], and so have remained unknown to most Armenians except for the few who have been able to find some of the better known ones. Only a few Armenians have even had the opportunity or interest to read some of these studies.

Among the illustrated European publications we have the following: (1) Tournefort, *Relation d'un voyage du Levant*, 1717; (2) Boré Rugène, *Aspect des ruines d'Ani*, 1843; (3) Homilton [*sic*— Hamilton, tr.], *Researches in Asia Minor, Pontus, Armenia etc.*, London, 1842; (4) Texier, Charles, *Description de l'Arménie la Perse et la Mésopotamie*, Paris, 1843; (5) M. Brosset, *Les Ruines d'Ani*, St. Petersbourg, 1860. In addition to these, other German and Russian scholarly travelers have brought out various publications about Ani which, however, thanks to Professor Marr's new excavations, have lost their timely appeal.

Among the Armenians, the prolific monk of Venice Fr. Ghevont Alishan's *Shirag* published in 1881 is a good text and is well known among Armenians, although it is dated now because of the new excavations. And, its illustrations are by Brosset, and since they are all drawings, they don't have the special intensity and liveliness of photographs. Furthermore, Fr. Alishan never visited Ani and relied more on European authors (Brosset and so forth). And there are also the works of Shahkhatunian and Archbishop Jalaliants whose studies of Ani were published almost half a century earlier and now seem more like antiquities. Nevertheless, they contain useful knowledge about the inscriptions, which is valuable because with the continuing collapse of the churches, the inscriptions are always eroding. Also, the albums of Ani by G[arabed] Basmajian and Arshag Fetvadjian are also available.

But the fact remains that after Professor Marr's recent excavations of Ani there is new work and knowledge for us all to gain a deeper understanding of Ani's history and present condition. Thus, I felt a sense of urgency in writing this book with the hope of (1) providing a guide to visitors of Ani and (2) familiarizing those who do not have the opportunity to visit Ani with as much knowledge as possible. I hope thus to awaken in the Armenian people an interest in visiting Ani and seeing with their own eyes this great museum of the art and crafts of Armenian antiquity.

In order to make my study accessible to the people, and to be clear, but in my own distinct fashion, I have divided *The Ruins of Ani* into four primary chapters.

1. History of Ani: In this chapter I note all the chief historical events of the Pakraduni period which have a close connection with the periods of the foundation, growth and prosperity, and destruction of Ani. My primary source for this is the multivolume *History* by Chamchian.

2. Topography of Ani: In this chapter I verify Ani's position—its distance from the nearby cities, the extent of its territory in meters. I have also added a plan of Ani, based on the one prepared by [H. F.] Lynch. I prepared this chapter as an eyewitness who has used his own research and Lynch's figures.

3. Description of the Ruins of Ani: This chapter is based on my own experience at Ani while traveling with the Catholicos on a journey that took us through St. Petersburg and the Caucasus. I give a full description of all of Ani's ruins with their inscriptions, for which I have used Archbishop Jalaliants's *Journey to Armenia*. This chapter was published in an abridged form under the pseudonyms "Northern Traveler" and "Hrayr" in the Armenian-language newspaper *Piwzantion* [Byzantium] [published in Constantinople, tr.] last year.

4. Scholarship on Ani: This chapter deals with Armenian architecture, and I survey the European scholarship about Armenian art and crafts. In the second section, which I hope is of contemporary appeal, I discuss Professor Marr's excavations, and use my own writings about my epic journey to Ani.

Because I hope that my study of Ani will appeal to a broader audience and be more vivid than previous ones, I have included in the text thirty-five photographs that I took last year, which I had prepared in Europe with great care. My hope is that they are richer and more vivid than any images of Ani that have yet been seen.

The present state of Ani as well as the state of the Armenians today reminds me of Dante's words: "What is more grievous and heartrending than to recall the glory of past days when one is living in days of misfortune." If it is grievous during times of failure and torment to recall the old days of glory, I would say that not only is it not grievous, but it is, on the contrary, consoling. It is consoling to recall those bygone days of Armenian glory and greatness. Ani is one of its living and eternal monuments. It is a work of Armenian genius, and the Armenian world can truly be proud of it.

It seems historically true to say that as brilliant, inventive and enterprising as Armenians might be as individuals, collectively, we appear to be inept. I think we can see in this problem our national misfortunes . . . because when Armenians, who have great individual talents, come together, they neutralize one another, and the result is negative.

If we look briefly at the last century of Armenian history, this becomes apparent. Was it not an illustrious Armenian who a few decades ago saved the Russian Empire from unprecedented anarchy during the last days of the Czar?[2] Were they not famous Armenian generals who occupied the inaccessible Caucasian mountains

---

2. Mikhail Loris-Melikov (1824–1888), a Russian-Armenian who was an important general, especially in the Russo-Turkish war of 1876, and later a

and curbed the rebellious tribes there, and in doing so, helped Russia add to its empire? Were there not very rich Armenian merchants who served as the guides for England's domination of India, which is the largest jewel in the English crown? Do Armenians not exist even today in European states who play active roles as ministers, senators, and high-level officials in Russia, Austria-Hungary, Rumania, Persia, and especially in Turkey, where during the last century such famous *amiras* performed great services for the Ottoman state during difficult, economically ruinous times?

Have we forgotten that more than ten Armenian Arshaguni [Arshakuni/Arsacid] emperors sat on the Byzantine throne, and that two warrior Armenian kings sat on the throne of Bulgaria? Isn't it true that, wherever the Armenian has been, has he not occupied a leading position as a government official, a martial and military general, a shrewd diplomat and ambassador, a resourceful merchant, an ingenious craftsman and artisan, a scientist in various fields, and of course as the pioneer of freedom in the East, and often at the cost of great sacrifices? Sacrifices which brought the Armenians to the threshold of death.

If the Armenians have such talent, then why are the Armenian people living in such misfortune? Perhaps for two primary reasons: First, the Armenians are dispersed: a people of barely three and one half million are scattered throughout Turkey, Russia, Persia, Europe, Egypt, America and other places, which is to say on all the continents of the world (scattered in an unparalleled manner) so that except for the Araratian (Yerevan) province, where the Armenians are a majority and constitute about 650,000, they don't form a majority in any place. The second reason is that we do not have a defined national policy.

Every Armenian has a special policy for himself according to his way of thinking. The direction changes when a catholicos, a patriarch, or an official national body is changed. Every Armenian has

---

high-ranking member of the Czar Alexander II's government, and minister of the interior who was involved in efforts toward constitutional reform.

a different starting point for a national future, and follows different paths. Our political parties also follow these changing and sometimes contradictory directions.

It is for these reasons that we attack each other and create disputes and divisions, and it is ironic because we are just starting to get out from under the despotism that has nearly destroyed us. As the new Turkish reforms attempt to ameliorate old conditions of tyranny, we seem to be heading down a road of national suicide and national dissolution. Let us hope that our own divisions, which have been so prevalent in the past two years during this moment of transitional Ottoman constitutional reform, will soon end so we can create a new invigorating era, and seek peaceful progress in education and our economy. This is the only path for our salvation.

This first monograph of mine gives me the opportunity to express, once more my deep filial gratitude to the beloved Patriarch of All Armenians His Holiness Matteos II, the Most Holy Catholicos, who among Armenian clergy in Turkey chose me as his companion in his historical journey, and gave me the good fortune to—among other things—see with my own eyes this temple of Armenian antiquity. In doing so I quenched a deep desire that I had had since boyhood to see Ani. As a small filial offering, I dedicate my modest study with eternal gratitude to his renowned Name.

Constantinople, April 2, 1910,
Very Rev. Fr. K. Balakian

CHAPTER I

History of Ani

Part I: The Founding and Flourishing of Ani

One of the glories of the royal house of the Pakradunis was the construction of the capital of Ani, which was known in its time as the city of a thousand and one churches. Of course, Ani did not have a thousand and one churches, but because Ani and the surrounding Shirag district had hundreds of churches, temples, and chapels, the designation was an emblem of the multitude of large and small places of worship that defined its landscape.

We know from Armenian history that King Drtad [Trdat] gifted the district of Shirag to the princely Gamsaragan [Kamsarakan] clan, which made this fertile district flourish and grow. The proverb of Shirag's fertility and Sharay's belly is recalled in particular.[3] Ashod Msager [Ashod the Meateater], the grandfather of the founder of the Pakraduni kingdom at the end of the eighth century, was so enchanted by this famous fertile place that he bought that district from the Gamsaragans and settled his family in Ani, which was then still a small and insignificant settlement. Gradually Ani grew and flourished thanks to the fertile lands of the surrounding

---

3. Translator: According to Movses Khorenatsi, the region of Shirag was given to Sharay, one of the gluttonous descendants of Hayk'. See *History of the Armenians*, ed. and trans. Robert W. Thomson (Ann Arbor: Caravan, 2006), 87.

district and the strength and impregnability of its natural position, so that during the time of Smpad [Smbat] II and Kakig I, it achieved the greatest fame and glory. Ani, with its fortified walls, marvelous royal palaces and princely mansions, its elegantly sculpted churches and impregnable high citadel, excited the envy and avarice of neighboring nations, especially because it enjoyed great renown as a rich and mercantile capital.

Both foreign and Armenian historians write with admiration and praise of Ani's affluence, the richness of royal and princely palaces, and the great population of the capital; they even claim that the population of Ani was as large as a million, which I think is an exaggeration, and I will write about this at length in the chapter on Ani's topography.

When Ashod I, founder of the Pakraduni kingdom, received royal status and garments from the *amira* of Baghdad through the mediation of the Seljuk osdigan Yise of Dvin in 885, he was consecrated as king by Catholicos Kevork II in the presence of Armenian *nakharars* [feudal lords], princes, and a great crowd of the people. In this fashion, according to the national historians, Ani became the capital of the Pakraduni kings. It was in that same year that the emperor of the Greeks, Basil Arshaguni, also sent a royal crown and scepter to King Ashod. Some, however, think that it was Ashod III the Merciful (952–977), the eldest son of King Apas [Abas] of the Pakradunis, who for the first time established his throne in Ani, and that it was he who turned Ani into the capital of the Pakraduni kings in his day. My own opinion is that this discrepancy of a century in time is the result of a confusion in names, and that it was Ashod I who, for the first time, was consecrated by Catholicos Kevork II in Ani. Consequently, I think that Ani became a capital from that time, 885, on.[4]

What is certain is that during Ashod III the Merciful's long reign Ani became stronger and more prosperous. It was he who built the famed citadel of Ani, which, thanks to its naturally inaccessible and

---

4. Translator: Most scholars maintain that it became the capital in 961.

Great Ararat 5,157 meters, Little Ararat 3,914 meters (Masis).

architecturally constructed position, was in its time truly considered impregnable. Queen Khosrovanush, Ashod the Merciful's wife, who built the marvelous monasteries of Haghpad and Sanahin, is well memorialized at Ani.

We know, as well, from history, that many of the famous buildings of Ani were constructed during Smpad II's reign as king (977–999). It was Smpad II, a great builder and the Pakraduni king, who commissioned and oversaw the massive walls along Ani's northern side with their semicircular, elevated towers and embankments—all of which he built in eight years. It was Smpad II who commissioned the famous architect Drtad to build Ani's renowned cathedral, which, with its interior hollow arches and sky-high dome, has been an achievement of great admiration and amazement for Armenian and European architects. Due to King Smpad's early death, however, the construction of the cathedral was completed by Kakig I's wife, Queen Gadranite [Katramide], whose special inscription I've made note of in my chapter.

What is also clear from Armenian history is that Ashod III the Merciful, this virtuous and high-achieving king who occupies a great place among the Pakraduni kings, was consecrated king in

Ani with great pomp by Catholicos Anania in 961, in the presence of King Pilibbos of the [Caucasian] Albanians and Catholicos Hovhannes.

King Kakig I's consecration in the Pakraduni capital is an important event in the history of Ani. During the reign of King Kakig I, Smpad II's brother and successor, Ani grew even more prosperous, strong, and powerful so that as an affluent, mercantile capital it aroused the envy of neighboring nations, especially the Greeks [i.e., the Byzantines, tr.], who became the first cause of Ani's destruction and decline.

Part II: The Sale of Ani

Hovhannes-Smbat, King Kakig I's eldest son, succeeded his prominent father in 1020. He proved to be an inept king; far from strengthening Ani, his weakness and lack of foresight were the cause of Ani's sale and surrender to the Byzantine emperor. It was during this period that sinister political clouds began to accumulate over Armenia, and from its distant corners the ill-boding news of invasions and oppressions reached Ani. The Seljuks, led by Tughril Beg, crossed the Tigris River and reached Mesopotamia, spreading destruction, and pillaging everywhere.

The bloodthirsty and ragtag multitude of Seljuks entered Armenia, first putting to the sword and flame Vasburagan, where the Ardzruni king Senekerim finally stopped the destruction and defended his country, thanks to his great general Shabuh and Senekerim's son Davit. Tughril Beg squashed Senekerim's resistance. He then attacked the Pakraduni king Hovhannes-Smbat III. Even though Hovhannes-Smbat sent his commander-in-chief Vasag Bahlavuni against Tughril Beg with his army, he fell victim to treachery and was killed, and the Armenians were defeated.

The Seljuk leader, Tughril, victorious in his first invasion, turned to Persia. He subjugated the country, restored the Persian kingship, and assembled new forces in preparation for his second invasion. King Senekerim of Vasburagan, terrified of the Seljuks, after negotiating with the Byzantine emperor Vasil [Basil] II, left his country to the latter; in return he received Sepasdia for his residence in 1021. It was in that year that Emperor Vasil invaded the Georgians with a great army in order to suppress the rebellion against his empire of the Georgian king Giorgi. Vasil II subjugated the latter in 1023 and began to approach Armenia's borders.

King Hovhannes-Smbat, who secretly had helped the rebellious Georgian king, seemed to lack the courage of most Armenian kings. Because he feared the vengeance of Vasil II, he sent Catholicos Bedros Kedatartz to be a conciliatory mediator to the emperor, and he promised in writing to give the royal capital of Ani to him after his death.

The Byzantine emperor was so happy about this unexpected act of generosity from the Armenian king (imagine giving away the great and rich capital of the Pakradunis), he took his army and left Armenia's borders. Even though he returned to his land, Ani's dark fate was already sealed. Vasil II died shortly thereafter and was unable to achieve his goal, but his successor, Emperor Gosdantin [Constantine VIII], who was a more conscientious ruler than his predecessor, on his deathbed (1029) summoned an unworthy priest named Giragos who had a connection with his court and entrusted him with King Hovhannes-Smbat's letter. He said to him: "Take this letter and give it to your king, and tell him that like all mortals, I too being on the threshold of Eternity, don't want to seize another's property. Let the King take back his kingdom and give his capital to his sons." But this cursed priest Giragos, instead of carrying out the wish of the benevolent Greek emperor, which would have saved his homeland, kept this royal letter decreeing the return of Ani and sold it for great profit to Emperor Gosdantin's successor, Emperor Michael V, in 1034. Thus Giragos became the cause of Ani's fall and destruction.

The ineffectual King Hovhannes-Smbat, who sold his kingdom and Ani in order to save his family, died in 1040. He was succeeded by Kakig II, son of his brother Ashod, who became the last ruler of the Pakraduni kingdom. But King Kakig II, though endowed with talent, was only a seventeen-year-old adolescent and in need of a guardian, and so Armenia descended into anarchy. In the wake of this, the Armenian *nakharars* began to fight one another. Encouraged by their fighting, Byzantine emperor Michael V sent ambassadors to Armenia demanding that Ani be surrendered to him in accordance with King Hovhannes-Smbat's promise. Although the Armenian *nakharars* and princes unanimously refused to comply, they were in such a state of chaos because of the divisions among themselves, they were incapable of resisting.

But out of this chaos, and through an unfortunate coincidence, as a result of Vesd-Sarkis Siuni's lust for glory and perfidious behavior, two parties emerged in Ani. As guardian of the underage King Kakig II, with his troops he seized the treasures and many of the cities and fortresses of the kingdom. He dreamed of becoming king of Armenia, and if he couldn't succeed, he would hand over Ani to the Byzantine emperor. Meanwhile commander-in-chief Vahram, who was Vasag Bahlavuni's brother and was faithful to the crown and king of the fatherland, wanted at all costs to defend the right of the legitimate heir to the kingdom and thwart Vesd-Sarkis's conspiratorial lust for power.

When the Greek emperor, Michael, saw that the *nakharars* would not willingly surrender Ani to him he was enraged; ready to use force, he sent three sets of troops to Armenia. Although they carried out much destruction and pillaging, they were not able to topple the city of Ani. Michael V, even more enraged by this failure, sent a fourth army of 100,000 men to besiege the city. At the same time, King Davit the Landless of the Albanians, upon the instigation of the Byzantine emperor, invaded Armenia and occupied the northwestern districts of the country.

The Greeks who were now camping in front of the ramparts of Ani, confident in their incomparable strength, rained insults and curses on the city dwellers daily. The Armenian commander-in-chief Vahram, who was a passionate patriot and wedded to his oath of loyalty, drove his troops—30,000 men—out of Ani's ramparts and fell upon the Greeks, who were overconfident in their might. Arrogant and unprepared, the Greek troops, terrified by the ferocity of the Armenian troops, panicked and fled in chaos, leaving over 20,000 wounded or dead. After this stunning victory, commander-in-chief Vahram Bahlavuni's partisans brought to Ani Ashod's son Kakig, who was the legitimate heir to the throne. There, in 1042, he was anointed King Kakig II by Catholicos Bedros Kedatartz in the cathedral of Ani. Kakig II, the last of the Pakraduni kings, was renowned for his wisdom and bravery.

When Vesd-Sarkis, Kakig's guardian, saw that his quest for conquest had not been realized, he fled, and fortified himself in the citadel of Ani. Kakig, the newly crowned and courageous king, went alone to the citadel without a single bodyguard. He persuaded Vesd-Sarkis to leave the citadel and the city of Ani. Though Sarkis was forced to withdraw to the Surmari fortress, he hadn't abandoned his plot against King Kakig, and so Kakig, with a small group, again advanced against the traitor, retrieved the royal treasures and fortresses from him, and imprisoned him in Ani. Vesd-Sarkis, however, pretending for the moment to be friends with the king, won many new allies like Krikor Makisdros [Grigor Magistros], who was the nephew of the commander-in-chief, and who now distanced himself from the king, even though Makisdros was the king's close advisor. During this period, he secretly incited Emperor Gostandin Monomachos, the successor to Emperor Michael V, to continue to pursue the conquest of Ani. When Emperor Gostandin Monomachos saw that King Kakig refused to bend to his demands, he sent Commander Michael Asit with a large army to Armenia with the hope of conquering Ani. Kakig fended off the Greek general, defeated the enemy's army, and returned victorious to Ani.

Upset by his defeat, Emperor Gostandin, on the one hand, after making preparations against the Armenian king, sent General Nigoghayos with a larger army, while with the other, enlisting the *amira* Apul-Suar of Dvin to attack the Armenians from the east. Kakig, however, without despairing or becoming confused, won Abul-Aswar to his side with expensive gifts, and then, with his entire army, attacked the Byzantine general Nigoghayos, who dared this time to attempt to become master of Ani. The fight did not last long, because the Armenians, animated in the defense of their capital city, defeated the Greeks, who quickly withdrew from Armenia's borders. Emperor Gostandin Monomachos, realizing now that he would not be able to occupy Ani by force, used his cunning and turned to Vesd-Sarkis because of his duplicitous relationship with his master.

The emperor wrote a friendly letter to Kakig, inviting him to Constantinople on the pretext of instituting a peace agreement. And to ensure his goal, Emperor Gostandin, in the presence of the delegates of the king of the Armenians, swore on the cross and the gospel to remain faithful to his promise. Nevertheless, King Kakig suspected a plot and refused the emperor's invitation. Vesd-Sarkis and his allies, however, along with Catholicos Bedros Kedatartz, worked on the king, pressing him to accept the Emperor's invitation and go to Constantinople, promising that they would remain faithful to him and would defend his throne and capital. To top it off, they pledged their loyalty to him in writing and even presented the document to him.

Although the Vahramian party expended all efforts to warn the king of the Byzantine conspiracy, and the deceit of Vesd-Sarkis's party, King Kakig was mostly taken in by Catholicos Bedros and ignored the Vahramian party's advice. Thus he went in royal splendor to Constantinople, taking with him [the fate of] his kingdom. Emperor Gostandin Monomachos hosted King Kakig with royal honors in his magnificent capital, and after a few days began to diplomatically demand Ani. When King Kakig categorically refused to surrender his capital, the emperor was enraged and imprisoned the Armenian king on one of the Marmara islands.

When a messenger arrived in Armenia with the bad news of Kakig's captivity, the *nakharars* met with Catholicos Bedros to deliberate. Some of the princes wanted to surrender Ani to Davit the Landless of the [Caucasian] Albanians, while others preferred King Pakarad of the Georgians and Abkhaz. Instead of deliberating on the means of defending and preserving the great capital of the Pakradunis against the enemy, these princes—these traitors to their nation—were thinking of ways to surrender Ani. And Catholicos

Bedros Kedatartz, instead of trying to save the royal throne and crown, did not want to miss an opportunity to satisfy his avarice, and so, through the Greek prince of Samosat, he sent Emperor Gostandin word that he was ready to surrender Ani if he would be given suitable compensation. Unfortunately, King Kakig, relying on the highest functionary of God, had handed over the forty keys of Ani to Catholicos Bedros, while the latter, unworthy of his grand predecessors, became the first betrayer of his homeland; he exchanged Armenia's crown, throne, and the capital of Ani to line his pockets with silver and gold. Armenia's crown and throne belonged to the people in common, but he chose the gold and silver which could only be his until his death.

After Gosdantin satisfied Bedros's greed, the unworthy Catholicos sent the forty keys of Ani to the emperor with a letter in which the *nakharars* and the Catholicos wrote: "We surrender Ani and all the eastern ancestral lands to the emperor." The misfortuned King Kakig, despite the betrayal of his *nakharars*, princes, and Catholicos, continued to resist, but to no avail; he was forced to carry out the illegitimate will of the emperor. He resigned from his royal throne in the year 1045, and in its stead received the city of Bizu in Cappadocia, where he married the daughter of King Davit of Sepasdia. But King Kakig, this last king of the Pakraduni dynasty, died tragically in Sepasdia, the victim of a Greek plot.

Emperor Gosdantin Monomachos sent the eunuch Parakamanos[5] with an army to Armenia to take over his new acquisition, Ani. When, however, he came to the walls of Ani he found the gates closed in front of him because the troops defending the city, united with the faithful citizens of the capital, were ready to defend their royal crown and throne and their beloved city. Barely had the Greek siege commenced when the Armenian troops, along with the citizens, attacked the army outside the walls and sent the Greeks fleeing Ani's borders. Then, however, the bad news arrived from Constantinople that Kakig had been forced from the throne and

---

5. Translator: The *parakoimōmenus*, a high-ranking Byzantine court position.

so could not return to Armenia. Upon learning this, the Armenian troops garrisoned at Ani were moved to unfathomable mourning. They found themselves completely deserted, surrounded by internal and external enemies, and they had no choice but to surrender. And so they called the Parakamanos back and surrendered Ani to him. In this way, the renowned royal residence and capital city of the Pakradunis, the city that had enjoyed great fame as a commercial, powerful capital, came to an inglorious end. Once more, that historical, great, but disastrous truth was confirmed—that more than the foreigner, Armenia's enemy has always been the Armenian. The pages of Armenia's national history are full of these examples. Was the kingdom of the Arshagunis not also destroyed through the Armenian *nakharars'* betrayal of their lords? Contrary to the great patriarch Sahag Bartev's vigorous resistance, they surrendered Ardashes, the last king [of this dynasty] to the Persians, claiming that he was too young and inexperienced to run the royal administration. They did not want to listen to the wise exhortations of the patriarch of blessed memory, and derided his words that "the sick sheep of the homeland is better than the healthy wolf of the foreigner." Are we not the original cause of the great part of the misfortunes which our nation has experienced, and should we not seek this cause among ourselves?

In this way, the Greeks were able, even if barely, to occupy Ani and the surrounding districts. They seized all the cities and fortresses while carrying out great brutalities. They removed the Armenian princes from their native lands and poisoned some of them. They even took Catholicos Bedros Kedatartz to Constantinople and did not spare him, even though he had given them Ani. Finally, the Greeks attempted through all imaginable means to liquidate the Armenian nation, with the goal of assimilating the Armenians among themselves.

Part III: The Seljuk Invasions and the Destruction of Ani

Tughril Beg, the leader of the Seljuks, invaded Armenia again. Blood and tears flowed in all the districts through which he passed.

After the death of the murderous Tughril, his brother Alpaslan [Alp Arslan], with all his troops and forces at his disposal, entered Armenia like a torrential flood. Advancing unobstructed, he came to Ani and besieged it with the hope of becoming master of the capital's wealth. The siege lasted a long time, during which Alpaslan, with his massive and terrifying catapults, destroyed part of the walls, but still he was unable to enter the city.

In despair, Alpaslan was at the point of leaving with his army when the princes and notables in the capital, thinking that the enemy was preparing a new attack, withdrew to the citadel. The populace, remaining undefended, panicked and began crying out. At this time, the Seljuks returned and fiercely attacked the city, entered, and began slaughtering the innocent inhabitants without sparing the elderly or children, virgins or youth, so that the waters of the Akhurian were bloody. They carried out such brutalities and unprecedented barbarities that we scarcely can find similar examples in history, except for those that are characteristic, generally speaking, of the Tatars. This destruction of Ani at the hands of Alpaslan took place in 1064, after which Ani was now prey to the enemies pouring into Armenia from all over, until its final razing to the ground, as we will see in the course of our story. After the destruction of the kingdom of the Pakradunis, Armenia fell into the hands of enemies and was divided up into pieces. Thus Ani, Dvin, and Gars became separate principalities. An *amira* sat in each of them, ruling over his tributary peoples. And, of all the cities of Armenia, Ani had the most volatile fate, with its richness and opulence always arousing the greed of conquering rulers.

After being subject to Alpaslan's wrath, Ani became the principality of a Turkish *amira* named Manuche [Minuchir/Manuchir], but it was Alpaslan's successor, Melikshah [Malikshah], who subdued Emir Manuche and brought Ani once more under his dynasty's rule. The successor of Melikshah, the weaker Apul-Suar, however, saw that he would not be able to maintain his authority against raids, and wanted to sell Ani to the emir of Gars. When the people of Ani learned of this, they asked for the protection of King Davit of Georgia, and so Davit came with troops and occupied Ani. He gave the cathedral, which the Persians had turned into a mosque, back to the Armenians, and, in 1124, taking Apul-Suar with him, put him in prison in Georgia.

Not long afterward, King Davit of the Georgians died, and Apul-Suar's eldest son and successor, Padlun [Fadlun], having received aid from the *amiras* of the area, arrived with his troops and besieged Ani. The people of Ani, led by their Georgian mayor, valiantly defended their old capital, and Armenian women were also part of this. History remembers the brave-hearted Armenian woman named Aydzeam, who never feared the arrows of the enemy. The siege lasted a long time. Padlun entered into negotiations with Ani's princes and notables, promising that if they surrendered he would keep the city at peace and prevent further bloodshed. As there was a scarcity of provisions in Ani, and no aid was arriving from the Georgians, the inhabitants of the city accepted their previous ruler (1126). Thus Padlun took all of Shirag [district] under his rule and governed peacefully until his death in 1132. The Georgians, however, during King Giorgi's reign, grew strong before long and invaded the Shirag district, then conquered Ani under Padlun's nephew (also named Padlun). Although the *amira* of Manazgerd had come with troops to support Ani's *amira*, in 1161 they were defeated badly by the Georgians.

The Georgian King Giorgi, encouraged by his victory, marched on Dvin and was victorious and then was merciless toward his defeated victims. In response to this, the king of Persia led a charge against the Georgians. He raided Shirag and the borders of Georgia for four years, so that Giorgi was forced to leave Ani to the Persians in order to acquire new forces. Giorgi then returned to seize Ani from the Persians, and, in 1174, handed over the governing of Ani to the Orpelian princes (of Georgia).

From the Far East, Genghis Khan, at the head of a multitude of hundreds of thousands of Tatars, after conquering China, India, and Persia, entered Armenia with formidable force. He inaugurated a new age of misery and misfortune in Armenia, which was now bereft of rules and already disrupted numerous times by the Tatars. The pages of [Armenian] national history do not bear a blacker and more fiendish inscription than that of the expeditions of Genghis Khan's Tatars. And, Genghis Khan's successor [Ogedei Khan] sent a large army under the commander Charmaghan to again conquer Ani.

When the people in the region of Ani heard that Charmaghan was approaching the city of Ani, they rushed in fear to take refuge inside the city walls with their belongings, with the hope that the enemy could not break them down. When the Tatar commander with his locust-like multitudes approached Ani, he sent a few emissaries to the residents of the city demanding that they surrender immediately. But the people attacked and killed the emissaries. Enraged by this, Charmaghan now planned to raze the city, and he besieged Ani with his formidable army. Due to the treason of some of Ani's notables, the siege of the city did not last long. When Charmaghan entered it, he ordered its inhabitants to be slaughtered mercilessly; he even had suckling babes drowned in pools of blood. His forces destroyed what they could through vandalism, including that of palaces, churches, and many other beautiful buildings. And what they could not wreck, they burned, pillaging Ani in unprecedented ways; such destruction and slaughter cannot be imagined. Ani and its environs were covered with piles of corpses, and those remaining alive took refuge in valleys and groves. The majority of Ani's population was dispersed, and women and girls were subjected to brutal cruelties. In 1239, most of the girls were taken captive.

Almost a century after this terrible invasion, in 1387 Tamerlane (Lengtimur or Timurleng), one of the scions of Genghis Khan, hoped to restore Genghis Khan's ruined state. He assembled hundreds of thousands of Tatars, and, leading this savage mob, set out from the capital of Samarkand on an expedition. He passed through India and Persia, leaving floods of blood behind him, entered Mesopotamia, conquered and destroyed Baghdad, burned Damascus, and after seizing Syria [lit. Asorik] from the hands of the Mamluks, victoriously entered Armenia, ferocious with a need to satiate his lust for blood. For five years Tamerlane trampled upon Armenia, making blood and tears flow everywhere. Ani was not spared its share of these bloody massacres, and it was finally leveled to the ground. Thus its centuries of glory were obliterated because of the massacres of the Genghis Khan–Tamerlane era.

Ani was condemned three times to terrible plunder and destruction: (1) during Alpaslan's time in 1064, (2) under Charmaghan's reign in 1239, (3) under Tamerlane's terror in 1387. During this last reign of terror, Ani was totally destroyed and became uninhabited. For nearly 150 years Ani had been a royal capital, and after the historic life it had had for nearly 450 years, it ceased to be an inhabited place. The bits and pieces of Ani's remaining populace were scattered throughout the world, in places like Russia, Emiret [Imereti], Crimea, Kazan, Poland, Romania, Bulgaria, and Greece.

Thus no stone remains on another in that famous royal capital of the Pakradunis. The old walls are largely destroyed, the royal palaces collapsed, [and] the fragrances of the princely gardens—where we do not find even one tree today—do not exist. It is as if Ani is surrounded by desert because not one spring brings water to it. These historical ruins today speak to the heart of the visitor who can't help but lament the centuries of sorrow that shadow the Armenians.

I hope this concise overview gives the reader a small sense of the founding, flourishing, and destruction of Ani.

CHAPTER II

Topography of Ani

Ani resides in the southern part of the Shirag district, fifty *versts* [c. 33 miles] from the city of Aleksandrapol [Alexandropol, now Gyumri], which means a carriage journey of four to five hours. Although Ani has a railway station of the same name barely two to three hours away, which is part of the railway line extending through Tiflis-Etchmiadzin-Yerevan, because means of transportation (carriage, horse) at the Ani station are not always available, visitors prefer to travel to the ruins via Aleksandrapol.

It is a ten-hour journey from Holy Etchmiadzin to Ani—five hours by railroad from Etchmiadzin to Aleksandrapol, and five more hours from Aleksandrapol to Ani, while it is fifteen hours from Tiflis to Ani—ten hours by railroad from Tiflis to Aleksandrapol, and five more hours by carriage from there to Ani. Ani is located in Shirag's plain, which stretches from Aleksandrapol to the south; it is uneven terrain near the wooden bridge of the Gars River, and as you approach Ani the terrain takes the form of a real cape, and turns into a promontory due to the surrounding deep valleys. This cape-promontory landmass of Ani's is only attached to the plain from the northeastern side and is defended by huge double walls and strong towers from the probable attack of the enemy. At the southeastern side, the Akhurian River (the Arpa Chay) flows quietly through the bottom passage of the rupture of an abyss at a depth of four to seven and more *gankuns* [around 6–10 feet], and sometimes rumbling, it twists its way down the winding valley, after uniting with the Gars River, pouring into the Arax [Aras River].

Although the Akhurian's valley is wedge shaped and deep like an abyss, and unapproachable by an enemy, our ancestors still surrounded this side with Ani's strong walls. Although the latter have now collapsed, their traces can still be clearly seen. From the west, Dzaghatzor Alaja riverlet, which is less deep and more accessible in comparison to the Akhurian's valley/gorge, flows sinuously. Dzaghatzor is also surrounded by walls whose traces are also still seen today. Dzaghatzor's Alaja riverlet makes a great semicircular arc near Ani's southwestern corner, and joins with the Akhurian River. The land/shore has taken the form of a pointed horn near this confluence which is the most distant point of this great cape. Aghchegay Pert [the Girls' Fortress] was built upon its inaccessible and deserted tall cliffs. The ruins of this fortress can be observed from the heights of the citadel, which leave a profound impression on the nature-loving visitor.

There are numerous natural and artificial caverns and caves in Dzaghatzor. Some of these were connected with one another by means of secret narrow passages at the time, and there are others which still are. When a visitor enters through the great gate of the northern walls, he finds in front of him practically an equilateral triangular promontory which rises gradually, and upon reaching the distant end of the cape, takes on the shape of a perfect hill. And here, you find Ani's famous citadel and one of the royal palaces which rises 120 meters above the Akhurian River.

Ani's promontory is almost 700 meters above sea level, which is about the same elevation as Etchmiadzin, and it is almost 1,400 meters from the citadel to the great walls that stand opposite, and this constitutes the longest side of the triangle, while the base is longer than 1,200 meters and is the length of the great walls. If you walk alongside the edges of the walls surrounding Ani, you can circle it in fifty minutes. According to this calculation, Ani's footprint encompasses an expanse of approximately 860,000 square meters.

The size of Ani's population during its height has been much debated by [Armenian] national and foreign historians. Scholars often describe Ani's wealth and opulence and princely palaces sometimes claiming that the population was a million, which is a huge exaggeration. Just as the Frenchman Eugène [*sic* Marie-Félicité] Brosset didn't believe that Ani had one thousand and one churches, I do not believe that Ani had a population of one million. In the period of its greatest splendor it could have had a population of 100,000.[6]

Visitors to Ani know that it would be impossible for a million people to fit inside the perimeter of the walls. As I noted, the walls have taken on the form of a triangular cape with the deep gorges of the Akhurian and Dzaghatzor, and so if you imagine European capitals as populous as this city, note that they occupy an expanse twenty times larger or more than Ani. Some think that the space inside the walls of Ani was allotted to royal and princely habitation, and at the same time was the center of the city's garrison, and correspondingly the people lived outside of the walls. But we know from history that when Ani was besieged by its enemies the people also took refuge behind the city walls.

Now, it is easy for us to suppose that the people of the capital also lived inside the walls of Ani, as did all the inhabitants of fortresses and cities encircled by walls of that time. Consequently the version of one million inhabitants is indefensible. In my opinion, Ani's population, due to its compact size, could not have been greater than 80,000. It is lamentable that contemporary historians do not give any definite figure for its population. This makes it very difficult, if not impossible, to make an accurate estimate.

The mountains, known as Alaja, are a few hours from Ani's northwestern side. In 1878, during the last Russo-Turkish war, the Ottomans endured a terrible defeat there at the hands of General

---

6. See Mikayel Chamchian, *Hayots Patmutiwn: Skzbits ashkhari minchev 1784 tvakane* [History of the Armenians from the beginning to the year 1784] (Venice: Mekhitarists), 851.

Lazarev, who was of Armenian nationality. Only the commander, Mukhtar Pasha, escaped the massacre thanks to his swift steed. Today the small Armenian villages of Jala, Arazin, and Khargov are just a few hours from Ani. There is also a village that goes by the name of Ani which is populated by Turks, and the village of Alaja is inhabited by Kurds, while Pagnan is inhabited by Yezidis. Aside from these six nearby villages, the surrounding areas of Ani have no other dwellings, and desolation and death are everywhere.

CHAPTER III

Description of the Ruins of Ani

The External Walls

These historic external walls appear from a distance as scattered black points. And as you walk toward them, the more powerfully does your curiosity burn, and soon you find yourself before powerful walls built with polished stones and high semicircular towers the likes of which you have never seen anywhere else.

We know from Armenian history[7] that Smpad II, one of the famous kings of the Pakradunis, took eight years to build the northern walls. If we compare Ani's walls with those of Byzantine Constantinople, we will see that in width and height the Byzantine walls in certain places can't compare with Ani's. The walls of Ani are much higher, even in their present state, despite their having largely lost [the pointed crenellations of the fortifications], more than did the walls of Constantinople. Except for the walls of Yedikule, the Byzantine walls were built with plain stone and mortar, while Ani's walls both externally and internally were built with large polished stones so that, even in its present state, the artistic craftsmanship of the walls still attracts the admiration of European scholars and travelers.

---

7. See Chamchian, *History*, 851.

The northwestern walls and towers.

A part of the external double walls and the ruins of what is thought to have been Ani's library.

The internal vaulted part between two towers of the external wall.

Starting at the eastern side, Ani's walls stretch toward the north, and then turn west to completely surround the city, from both the Akhurian ravine and the Dzaghatzor. Unlike the other sides, the northeast, as it is the side of the shore, is not defended naturally either by rivers or deep gorges and is exposed to the attack of the enemy. Thus the walls there were built double, and the city is defended by powerful semicircular walls which protrude outward.

The walls of the Dzaghatzor and Akhurian ravines are almost completely destroyed, so that only their traces can be seen here and there. You see the remaining traces of this sort of wall particularly on the northeastern side, near the citadel, and at the edges of the ravine of the two-story ruined bridge of the Akhurian. The visitor's first profound impression comes from the encounter with the huge external walls that are nearly complete and with the numerous towers at the northeastern side. On them appear special window-like openings, which were sometimes used for observing the enemy and shooting arrows at them. In many spots on these walls of polished stones, there are patterns, including those of crosses made by black and white stones that disclose how much artistic care our ancestors

The ruins of the northern external wall.

put into these walls. Perhaps it is for this reason that the construction of these walls took several decades.

The height of the walls, even today, is about 4 to 6 meters, depending on the location, while the height of the towers is practically double that. It has been conjectured that during the period of the city's prosperity, which is to say before the walls had collapsed, their original height was 6 to 8 meters, and the towers were 8 to 12 meters, which is not a height to be derided. If the stones found near the base of the walls, which had fallen from the top, were to be reintegrated, the walls would certainly have a taller appearance.

It is thanks to these huge, solid walls and towers that Ani resisted the powerful enemies that attacked it from all sides. Although large Greek (Byzantine) and Tatar armies with hundreds of thousands of troops besieged Ani for months, they were not able to break into the city and were only able to gain control of it through the treachery of princes who deceived their masters. It is worth noting also that on the area of the plain of Shirag where the danger was greatest, the walls were double, making an attack of the enemy impossible from that side. As with all old fortress towns, there was at one

The main gate to the external wall.

time a large moat in front of the walls, but as Asoghig has noted they are all covered over now.

These huge exterior walls have several gates. The chief one of them is the Avak [Principal] Gate, and not far from there is the Dvin Gate. Between the two highest towers at the left side of the Principal Gate is the Gars [Kars] Gate, and there are a few smaller gates too, which were at one time built for the daily needs of the soldiers garrisoning the city. The Gars Gate on the eastern wall, is the most beautiful and ornamented of them. It has huge arches between two lofty towers and has a special architectural value. The continuation of the wall is still standing at this gate and has small patterned squares of black and white stones that have been beautifully designed, and also has an image of a lion carved on it.

On the wall on top of the Yerevan Gate of the eastern wall the following inscription is found:

In the year 769 (1320), by the grace and compassion of God, I Sargis Tsiments, customs official, leave to Saint Grigor of this Arjuarij the large and small portion for the peace of our patron Shahnshah

The Yerevan gate of the eastern wall.

and long life to his God-given children Zakaria and his brothers. If anybody obstructs this—my memorial—may he be anathematized by the all-powerful God; the firm observers will be blessed by God.[8]

European and Armenian architects have praised, in particular, these towers, which are close to one and other and which appear as great semicircular arcs from the outside, while others have the form of huge quadrangles. The walls from the inside have been dexterously joined together with arches—as is evident from the photograph—often in walls over 2 to 3 *arshins* [arshin: 2 1/3 ft, hence 4.6–7 ft] thick, and there are often secret passageways which ascend to the top of the towers, that were most likely observation points. They are wonderful constructions, which despite the various destructions over the long centuries are still standing and are even dominant in today's ruined condition.

---

8. Translator: For a different version, see H. A. Orbeli, compiler, *Divan hay vimagrutyan* [Corpus of Armenian inscriptions], vol. 1, no. 6, ed. B. N. Arakelyan (Yerevan: Haykakan SSR Gitutyunneri Akademia, 1965), 3.

The Cathedral

The cathedral (989–1001)[9] or principal church, which has always earned the special admiration of visitors because of its marvelous architecture, stands inside the walls and is situated toward the eastern side, not far from the ravine of the Akhurian.

King Smpad II, whom I noted earlier, had the foundation of the cathedral built in 989 by the hands of the famous architect Drtad. But, it remained half finished because of Smpad's death, and so Kakig I's wife, Queen Gadranite, completed it in 1001, as you will see in the inscription below. This was the same Drtad who built the cathedral and also oversaw the restoration of the magnificent Hagia Sophia church of Constantinople.

[Ani] Cathedral is 32 meters long and 20 meters wide, and, as can be seen from the photograph, is completely made with polished stones. Curved arches adorned with carvings appear on the outer walls which protrude outward and rest on top of the long pilasters set into the walls. These walls were built in order to prevent the huge walls from collapsing, as well as to generate an aesthetic brilliance.

Like the majority of the oldest Armenian churches, the cathedral had at its peak a glorious dome like that of Holy Etchmiadzin's cathedral; now as you can see in the photograph, it is completely destroyed. Although the four lateral walls of the church rise up straight (see photo), the roof is in four sections, and covered with large polished stones, as are the roofs of all such antique buildings. As the roof of the church is firmly established on four internal columns and four arches, it has remained standing until today. When we enter from the great door adorned with carvings, on the south side, we find four huge stone columns whose tops are connected to one another by arches and serve as the base of the church's dome. These columns are refined, very tall, and beautiful in their simplicity.

As you can see in the photo, the cathedral's interior is made of large polished stones and appears to be more impressive than the outside. These four huge columns are connected to one another by

9. See Chamchian's *History*, 851.

The cathedral viewed from the southeast, built in 989–1001 (32 by 20 meters).

The inner portion of the cathedral, which is vaulted and adorned with columns.

four arches and rest on plain capitals. Despite their centuries-old antiquity, the four external lateral walls of the church, as well as the four twin pillars and four arches inside, today remain standing unchanged. Because Drtad designed these huge arches to be hollow inside and because he made sure the columns were bearing only moderate weight, he engineered a concept that enabled the cathedral to withstand earthquakes and other kinds of physical attacks.

If other such old constructions from centuries ago have fallen into ruins, the reason is more that the columns were not built to bear the weight of the arches, and the arches were not able to support the weight they bore. The secret of the architect Drtad's wisdom must be noted here. It is possible to make a voyage through this famous cathedral's arches and the secret internal passages covered with stone, all of which have greatly impressed scholars who have visited here. Although Holy Etchmiadzin's cathedral is built in the same style, its vaults are full, and its columns short and thick, while the columns of this cathedral of Ani are both more delicate and taller, so that the ceiling connected by vaults is much higher. This gives the temple a majestic appearance.

The cathedral has two great doors and six large and eight small windows. We stress the large size of the windows in particular because the windows of the historical ruins of the Ararat plain and Shirag district, as well as all others in this area, are narrow and small, barely half a *kangun* width and one and one half a *kangun* length [c. 9 by 27 in]. Consequently all the old sanctuaries were very dark, while the interior of this cathedral, with three times the number of windows, and much larger in size, is bright and venerable. The bema (raised section) of the chief altar is 1 meter above the floor, like the bemas of the altars of all old churches. There is only one altar in the sanctuary [*khoran*[10]], and there one can see the large niches carved for each of the twelve apostles.[11] All of the ancient churches

---

10. Translator: The space in churches architecturally known as the apse or conch.

11. Translator: There are actually only ten niches.

that I've seen have only one main altar and no side altars. Other than this cathedral, according to the Mayr Mashtots [ritual book] there are no traces of fourteen consecrated stones on the walls and columns of other churches. Of course it is impossible to know whether there are consecrated stone crosses under the foundations of other churches. Nor have I seen in any of the old churches I've visited a baptismal font. Consequently we can surmise that only moveable stone fonts were used in the old times, such as the one I saw in the ruins of Zvartnots Church near Holy Etchmiadzin. Also, here at Ani, the remnants of a secret treasury are still visible in the sanctuary, where the church's sacred vessels and invaluable vestments were most likely kept. We know from Armenian history that during the construction of the cathedral, the seat of the Catholicate of the Armenians was transferred to Ani in 903 [*sic* 993].

Only the following inscriptions can shed a true light upon these ancient ruins. Thus on the southern wall of the cathedral, this inscription reads precisely:

In the year 450 of the Armenians [AD 1001], and 219 of the Romans [Greeks/Byzantines], in the time of the honored by God [and] spiritual lord Sarkis Catholicos of the Armenians and the glorious kingship of Kakig [I] of the Armenians and Shahan Shah [King of kings] of the Georgians, I Kadratine [*sic*] queen of the Armenians, daughter of Vasak, king of Syunik, took refuge in the mercy of God and by decree of my husband Kakig Shahan Shah, built this holy cathedral, which was founded by great Smpad, and we erected the house of God, a revived and living spiritual offspring, and a perpetual monument; and I embellished it with precious ornaments, gifts to Christ from me and my family, and sons Smpad, Abas and Ashot; you are commanded by me, Lord Sarkis servant of the church, after the death of this pious queen, to conduct at Vartavar,[12] [and] Hisnak [Advent],[13] forty-one [days of service for the dead] unceasingly until the coming of Christ; if anybody takes that

12. Translator: A special rite, with ancient origins, celebrated on the Feast of the Transfiguration.

13. Translator: In the Armenian church, the fifty-day period prior to the Nativity and Theophany of Christ.

inscription as unreal, let him be condemned by Christ to six 1433
months with Adam, in the year 1012 of God taking human form . . .
when believing in Christ of the Armenians this colophon was written by my own hand.[14]

It is confirmed by this inscription that Kakig I's wife Queen
Gadranite completed the cathedral in 1001, as I previously noted.
And, the following inscription can be read on the wall of the door
on the southern side:

In the year 662 (1213)[15] by the will of God I Dikran servant of Jesus
Christ built with my lawful wealth these stairs of this glorious holy
cathedral, which after many years were in ruins, and gave as presents to the holy cathedral from my treasury the store[16] in Kagdnots
two [books of] festivities and Saint Krikor one by one and two silver *skih*[17] of the chief altar, and I placed the yoke on the attendants
[of the church] to celebrate mass in my name every year until the
coming of Christ.[18]

It is understood from this inscription that a wealthy believer
named Dikran, seeing in 1213 that the cathedral needed renovations,
had repairs done and had this inscription written in order for his
memory to be blessed by future generations. On the western side,
to the left of the door we read the following inscription:

Through the will and mercy of beneficent God, I Aron Makisdros,
honored by glorious kingdoms with beautiful ornaments, and
while young, came to the east to the well-built fortress in Ani. I
raised all its walls with a mass of pillars, and well-fastened solidity;
and with my expensive treasures I brought with effort abundantly

---

14. Translator: For a different version, see Orbeli, vol. 1, no. 101, p. 35.

15. Dates in the Armenian calendar have been converted to those of the
Christian era.

16. Կողպակն = store.

17. An old measure of weight. [Translator: But it also means chalice in Classical Armenian.]

18. Translator: For a different version, see Orbeli, vol. 1, no. 100, p. 35.

flowing water into this fortress for the happiness and refreshment of the thirsty; and I brought with a gold ring reverence of the born-to-the-purple independent queen, from the fate [*sic*—tax, tr.] of the houses of this city and castes [?], which from year to year was 1 ½ liters, but upon the request of these subjects they abolished [it], and the finding of two liters, which (all this) the *Mutayib* gave.[19]

As we can see from this inscription, a very rich prince named Aron[20] Makisdros, honored by kings, had the ramparts built. However, it appears that what he is referring to are the ramparts near the citadel, to which he recalls in particular having water brought. Unfortunately because the date is illegible, it is difficult to historically ascertain the identity of the aforementioned Prince Aron. Other inscriptions also exist, but as they do not shed new light on what we know, I'm omitting them here.

On special days, worship services are conducted in the cathedral, and visitors to Ani come to give their oaths recalling, of course, the murmurs of that prayer and the halleluiahs and chanting of the Psalms through which our ancestors in those days made these magnificent arches and dome reverberate.

St. Krikor [St. Gregory] the Illuminator Church

St. Krikor the Illuminator Church (Nakhêshlu Kilise)[21] (1215) sits just a hundred steps away from the cathedral, toward the valley of the Akhurian. It is the most remarkable of all the churches of Ani because of its delicate exterior and interior carvings and paintings

---

19. Translator: This inscription has been transcribed in a different fashion by other scholars. See Orbeli, vol. 1, no. 107, p. 38, and H. M. Bartikyan, "Aharon Magistrosi ardzanagrutyan (1055–1056) mej hishatakvats harkeri masin," *Patma-panasirakan handes* [Historical philological journal] 1959, vol. 4, pp. 168–173.

20. Translator: Or Aran, which is a corruption of the name Aharon or Aaron.

21. Translator: In modern Turkish Nakışlı Kilise, meaning the ornamented or decorated church.

St. Krikor the Illuminator Church (Nakhêshlu Kilise), built in 1215.

and frescoes. The Turkish inhabitants of the area call this church the Nakhêshlu Kilise. Although St. Krikor the Illuminator Church is not as large or tall as the cathedral, it has remained more intact, perhaps because it is in a valley and it has been less visible to invaders and enemies over the years. Now, according to a preserved inscription, this church was built in 1215 by Sulimay's son Smpad, and was called from the start—Honents.[22]

Although this church is smaller than the cathedral and can barely hold a hundred people, it is even more beautiful, because its columned and sculpted dome is still fully intact and this gives the church a magnificent appearance both inside and out. The architectural style of the church is the same as that of the cathedral. Its four walls are entirely standing and its stone-covered roof is undamaged. Only the narthex with connecting arches has collapsed. As the photograph shows, the southern and northern walls

22. Translator: The name of the patron of this church is generally considered to be Tigran Honents. See for this monument Jean-Michel and Nicole Thierry, *L'Église de Saint-Gregoire de Tigran Honenc' a Ani (1215)* (Louvain-Paris: Peeters, 1993).

are ornamented like those of the cathedral with eleven delicate pilasters and sculpted arches, which are joined to each other. Each column's capital presents the images of different animals: lion, elephant, tiger, wolf, bear, sheep, goat, and deer, etc., and they have been so skillfully carved that it is easy to determine the type of animal at a glance.

Each carved stone of this church, built of polished and uniform stones, bears the letter Ա, Բ, Գ, or Ե, and so on [A, B, G, E and the succeeding letters of the Armenian alphabet, tr.]. Consequently we can assume that the sculptures of each of these stones were separately carved, and in order not to create confusion for the stonecutters, they added the characters before they placed the stones in their present positions. Otherwise, at the height of the capitals, it would have been difficult to carve in such a delicate fashion images of flowers and animals on stones.

The windows of this church are very narrow; barely 20 centimeters wide and 80 centimeters high. The eight windows of the dome are oval and small, as a result of which, like in all old buildings, the interior of the temple is very dark. Nonetheless the visual interior, or *nakhesh* [Turkish for decorations; images, tr.], as the locals say, of this church is wonderful. The various torments that the Holy Illuminator underwent are elegantly painted in frescoes on the walls and the inside of the dome in vivid, beautiful colors. We also see King Drtad on horseback with huge bracelets, which according to Professor Marr are the symbols of rule characteristic of ancient rulers. The picture of Nunē the virgin, one of the first martyrs, and the marvelous vision of the Illuminator—how Jesus the Only-Begotten, descended through rays of light to the Araratian plain, strikes the spot of the present cathedral, shaking the ground with a golden hammer, and Sandaramet—are beautifully depicted on the arches and the aforementioned walls of the interior. The Transfiguration of the Mother of God and the many manners of painful torments endured by St. Hripsime, one of the early martyrs, and her companions, are depicted in such vivid postures that it makes your hair stand up.

An example of the external carvings of the church.

It is not possible to see these images and not marvel. They are made with such delicacy and skill that in a single glance one can ascertain their depth and antiquity.

Although the church of St. Krikor the Illuminator resembles the cathedral on the outside, internally, it doesn't because while the cathedral's ruined dome is built on four huge columns and four great arches, there are no columns at all inside and the dome rests on only four great arches. As in the cathedral, the chief altar of this church is adorned with ecclesiastical vessels and decorations so that services can be conducted on special days.

The following inscription is found on the facade of the southern wall of this church:

> In the year 664 [1215], by the mercy of God, when the powerful master of the universe *amirspasalar*[23] and *mandaturtukhutses*[24] Zakaria

---

23. Translator: Commander-in-chief of the Georgian army.
24. Translator: In Georgian, *mandaturt-ukhutsesi*—grand marshal or lord high steward.

[Zakare] and his son Shahnshah became masters of this city of Ani, I Dikran, servant of God, son of Sulem of the Smpadawrents, of the Honents clan, for the sake of the long life of my lords and their sons built this monastery of St. Krikor, which used to be called Mother of God of the Chapel, which was at a precipice and with wooded places, which I bought with my legitimate treasure from the hereditary owners, and by means of much labor and treasure I enclosed this church with a wall all around. I built this church in the name of Saint Krikor the Enlightener and adorned it with many ornaments, with symbols of salvation, with holy crosses of gold and silver, and painted images, adorned with gold and silver and jewels and pearl, and with lanterns of gold and silver, and with relics of the holy apostles, of the martyrs, and with part of the dominical cross that has received God, and with all kinds of utensils of gold and silver, and with numerous ornaments. I built all kinds of habitations for the monks and princes, and arranged in them priests who celebrate the mass of the body and blood of Christ to perform mass without obstruction for the long life of my lords Shahnshah and his sons, and for the absolution of my sins; and I gave this gift to this monastery of St. Krikor land which I had bought with treasure and by decision of the masters of the land, and which I had built from the foundation . . . [here follows a long list of gifts given to the monastery by Dikran]. Now, if any of the great or small of my [people] or of foreigners attempt to obstruct what is written in my inscription, or usurp things from the products which are established in it, or obstruct the memory of this sinning servant of God for any reason, let such an individual be excluded from the glory of the son of God and inherit the punishment of Cain and Judas on his person and be anathematized by the three holy councils and the nine orders of angels and be responsible for our sins in front of God; and those who are obliging and keep firm are blessed by God. Israegh [Israel] the Scribe.[25]

As we can see from this inscription, the very wealthy Smpad son of Sulimay [Sulem] appears to have built, or more precisely, to have

---

25. Translator: As the transcription in Balakian did not fully make sense, I used the version in Orbeli (vol. 1, no. 188, pp. 62–63).

renovated and adorned this old church of the Enlightener built by Honents, and by donating properties to it, assured the provisioning of the church.

Church of the Holy Savior

The Church of the Holy Savior (966) is only a few dozen feet and ascending in elevation from St. Krikor the Illuminator Church. It was built by Marzpan Aplgharip [Abugharib], the son of Prince Krikor, who by deeding its properties, assured its splendor. This temple is built in a very different architectural style from the two churches I have previously described because it has the form of a circular polygonal tower, while the others and generally the majority of ancient churches have the form of regular quadrangles.

Inside it is one story, but outside it is two stories. The polygon of the lower story is formed by sixteen arcaded and carved split columns, which, in addition to serving as fortification for the building, give the temple a beautiful appearance. Despite the second or upper floor being smaller, it is composed of twenty arcaded and more refined twin columns with plain capitals. Between the columns both in the lower and upper stories are high narrow windows built in the style characteristic of ancient [Armenian] architecture. In this way the lower part, according to old custom, is very dark, so that without the light of a lamp it is impossible to conduct services or any sort of reading. As is seen in the picture, the stone dome is still completely standing, and only some stones have fallen due to the destructive course of time. It has only one door which is half buried under stones which have fallen from the roof. On the left side of this door, a little above it, one can read the following inscription:

In the years of the divinely honored spiritual Lord Bedros Catholicos of the Armenians, and during the kingship of Smpad's son's Kakig Shahnshah in the year 455),[26] I Aplgharip Marzpan, son of

26. Translator: The date in the Armenian calendar of ՆԾԵ, or 455, would be 1006 in the Gregorian calendar which we use today in the West, but is

Church of the Holy Savior, built in 966.

Prince Krikor and grandson of Apughamr and brother of Vahram and Vasag, built this Holy Savior church in this capital of Ani with much effort and expensive treasure; I built from my legitimate possessions a certain store and olive-press, and my vineyard and *holavor*[27] and I gave [them] to this Holy Savior church, which I ornamented with gold and silver and precious gems, and I gave the Gospel and a *tavnagan*[28] for which I chose readings from the Old and New Testaments, and placed this before my Savior; now if anybody, either the mighty or the insignificant, [opposes] my expressions or other things which I have given and if they steal them,

---

converted incorrectly to 966 by Balakian. However, most other scholars read the date as ՆՁԵ, or 485, which would correspond to the year 1036 of the Gregorian calendar (see Orbeli, no. 126, pp. 44–45, or A. Manucharyan, "Anii S. Prkich ekeghets u shinararakan erku ardzanagrut yunnere" [Two inscriptions concerning the construction of the church of Surb Prkich at Ani], *Patma-panasirakan handes* [Historical-philological journal], 1976, no. 4, pp. 243–246).

27. Arm.: հոլավոր. Meaning unknown. Perhaps a kind of storehouse, as from *holem/holonem* (to gather, collect).

28. Translator: A collection of commentaries for feast days.

may they be prohibited, may they be anathematized by the 318 patriarchs . . . from this my world, I oblige the servants [of the church] and . . . be carried out unobstructed during the day of Vardavar'.[29]

From this inscription, it is clear that the Church of the Holy Savior is one of the oldest churches of Ani, built in 966 [*sic* 1035] by Marzpan Aplgharip, son of Prince Krikor. In accordance with the virtuous tradition of the old princes, he endowed and adorned this church that he built with his movable and immovable possessions and precious sacred vessels and manuscripts. He also donated an olive press which now during excavations has been uncovered. It should be noted that such oil presses, which at the time prepared the indispensable oil for church rituals, are often discovered during excavations.

In addition to this inscription, the following one can be read on the northern wall of the church:

In the year 414 (965),[30] I, Marzpan Aplgharip brought an edict from Smpad Shahnshah to the Emperor of the Greeks in Constantinople and with great effort and expensive treasure a part of the Holy Cross. Having come I completed this temple and erected the sign of light as a crown of the bride of Christ, and placed the yoke on the servants of the church to conduct the night service on Sunday until the coming of Christ, and if a priest of the Holy Savior church dies they should have 40 prayers in this church. And if any of the priests usurps my vessels or books of this church or by spending or any reason or through avarice go back and steal the revenue of this church [and] not use them for the need of this Holy Savior church, may he be anathematized by the 318 patriarchs, and he who removes the sons of Krikor the priest from church wardenship be doubly

29. Translator: For other versions of this inscription, see Orbeli, no. 126, pp. 44–45, or A. Manucharyan, "Anii S. Prkich ekeghetsu shinararakan erku ardzanagrut yunnere," *Patma-panasirakan handes* [Historical-philological journal], 1976, no. 4, pp. 243–246.

30. Translator: Again, this date is given differently by other scholars as 484 (A.D. 1035). See Orrbeli, vol. 1, pp. 45–46.

subject to curse, while may those who carry it [this writing] out be blessed; remember Kevork the writer to the Lord, amen.

It can be derived from this inscription too that Marzpan Aplgharip, who erected the Holy Savior Church in 966, went to Constantinople one year prior to the construction of the church, that is, in 965, with the royal edict of King Smpad of Armenia, or, as per the inscription, Smpad Shahnshah,[31] and presented himself to Michael, emperor of the Greeks, and through great effort and expense brought a small piece of the Holy Cross to Ani. Building this church, he kept that dominical holy relic there; because of this, he called the church Holy Savior.

In all inscriptions of this type there are always instructions for the functionaries of the church to conduct services on special days until the coming of Christ. It is as if these worthy princes never imagined that their much-celebrated capital city could be destroyed many centuries before the coming of Christ . . . and even turned into a pile of ruins. Either these princes thought the coming of Christ to be imminent, as they were probably influenced by the rumors and hopes circulating about Christ's coming in the year 1000, or they were simply arrogant in thinking that their capital was inviolable. Whatever it might have been, it appears from their inscriptions that they were men of virtuous minds and pure hearts to have thought and written what they have here.

Church of the Holy Apostles

The Church of the Holy Apostles (1000), found practically in the center of the city, is one of the oldest churches of Ani. This church is famous for its beautifully built and elegantly carved door, constructed in the Arabian style.[32] No other church has ornamentation like it. It is built with three domes, which now are partially

---

31. Shahnshah means king of kings.

32. Translator: Here the author refers to the narthex or gavit of the church, which was added to the church sometime before 1215, the date of its earliest inscription.

Main door of the Church of the Holy Apostles, built in 1000.

collapsed. The visitor is amazed at with what care and skill these massive monolithic stones were raised on these high walls. As in the Kagkashen [built by Kakig] Church of St. Krikor, here too there are beautifully carved capitals in the form of eagles.[33]

The Church of the Holy Apostles seems to have been built in the year 1000, and it was the famous seat of the Bahlavuni bishops. Today, the tomb of Catholicos Parsegh can be found near the church. During this period, even though the Patriarchate of All Armenians resided in Cilicia, the two sees of the Armenian Church were on good terms with each other.

There are inscriptions on the temple wall on the gate side, and the most interesting of them is written on the western arch.

In the year 769 (1322)[34] by the grace of God, I Khuandghes, spouse of Atabek Shahnshah, who this year left this world, sorrow was great

33. Translator: This is unprecedented testimony of eagle capitals both at the Holy Apostles Church and at Kagkashen, following the model, Balakian tells us, of the seventh-century church of Zvartnots.

34. Translator: The conversion of the date to the Gregorian calendar should be 1320, not 1322.

among us and the Eastern world, I the wife of Shalatin Sahipti Paron Zakariay,[35] for the sake of the salvation of the Patron's soul and the long life of my brothers, we have in our native city of Ani—remitted taxes on cows and donkeys, as well as large and small entry permits (?), [whosoever] tries to oppose this,[36] whether he be Armenian or Georgian, or Tajik[37] [may he] be condemned by God, share in the fate of Satan and be his companion in Hell, may the Georgian be excommunicated and damned, be companion in the hell of Satan, and the Georgian be [. . .[38]] and be damned; let the Tajik be covered with shame and found guilty before the glorious prophets of God, while those who firmly keep these injunctions until the end of the world, be blessed by the Almighty; let those who oppose these my words be anathemized as Judas and Cain; these good works and charity were established under the governance of the Baron Pilip. Bdugh, scribe."[39]

Aside from this confused inscription there is also the following writing on the western column of the temple.

In the year 750 (1311)[40] by the grace of God I Arpughes son of Khane, grandson of the great Zakaria, came to Ani on the command of

---

35. Translator: According to the Orbeli version, this last clause begins "I his wife, daughter of Shamshadin Sahipdivan and Paron Khawshak, grandchild of Atabek Ivane, and my son Zakaria" (Ōrbeli, vol. I, p. 27).

36. Translator: *zanhavats khap anel*—this version doesn't fully make sense, but an alternate version would be translated as "suppress our legacy" (Orbeli, 27).

37. Translator: Tajik can mean a Muslim, though after the coming of the Seljuks and Ottomans it was also used for Turks. See Hracheay Acharyan, *Hayeren armatakan bararan* [Dictionary of Armenian root words], vol. 4 (Erevan: Erevani Petakan Hamalsaran, 1979), 365–366.

38. This is a contemptuous word which we have omitted as contrary to propriety. [Translator: the word *krul*, which Garabed Basmadjian translates as "excommunicate" (see G. Basmadjian, *Les inscriptions d'Ani, de Bagnair, et de Marmachen* (Paris: Firmin-Didot, 1931), 368–369)].

39. Translator: For an alternative transcription accepted by most scholars, see Orbeli, vol. I, p. 27. This translation draws from Basmadjian's French translation in *Les inscriptions d'Ani*, p. 369.

40. Translator: This date should be 1301 in the Gregorian calendar.

The inscriptions of the southern side of the Church of the Holy Apostles.

Shahnshah, [and] saw this city, impoverished and left in great ruin, because great taxes were imposed on it, which never had occurred from the beginning. I suppressed three taxes for the sake of the life and health of my brothers Shahnshah and me, and for the tomb of my ancestors. I left a count of nine thousand cows; sheep, *aghlhargn*[41]; if anybody is of my race or any other, if he keeps my memory constant, he will be blessed by God the omnipotent.[42]

This inscription is important because it confirms that Ani was an important city until 1311, and contrary to what has been generally thought, it was not destroyed in 1064. It is true that on the latter date Alpaslan came and sacked Ani, and victoriously invaded its ramparts and spread ruin everywhere. However, after this Ani remained intact for a long time—for over three hundred years—until the invasion of Tamerlane, after which the city became an uninhabited place.

---

41. Translator: If this word is actually *aghlhargn* (classical aghlharkn), it would mean a tax on sheep.

42. Translator: For a different version, see Orbeli, 28.

But we can see from this inscription, that Arpughes, the son of Khane and the grandson of the famous Zakaria, came to Ani upon Shahnshah's command. This Shahnshah cannot be the king of kings of the Armenians, of course, because the Pakraduni kingdom was long destroyed. He must have come on behalf of the Georgian king, as he testifies, "I came [and] saw this city impoverished and left in ruin the scale of which had never occurred before."

This inscription casts much light on the last years of Ani, but, alas, the stones of these inscriptions are on the verge of eroding.

However, there are four more inscriptions in addition to the ones above, but I'm not quoting them here because they do not provide any new insights about the past. They simply note the donation of several stores or a field and thus ask for a mass to be held for their souls on special days which they specify.

The Apughamrents Church of St. Krikor [St. Gregory]

Not too distant from the Church of the Holy Apostles, at the edge of Dzaghadzor,[43] are the abutments of Apughamrents Church of St. Krikor. Drtad, the famous Armenian architect of the main cathedral, also built this church at the expense of Prince Krikor Bahlavuni nearly twenty years before the occupation of Ani by Alpaslan—in 1040, as the inscription confirms.

This Church of St. Krikor was built in the architectural style of the Church of the Holy Savior, and is polygonal (twelve sided or dodecagonal). However, it does not have columniated arches on its exterior walls as the Holy Savior church does, and is smaller, circular, and with a dome that is arcaded and columniated. It still remains standing with its pointed peak, [for] which is [it is] thought to be a tomb. Although its windows are narrow and high like those of the Church of the Holy Savior and the other churches, they are more beautiful, and are framed with pilasters and semi-arches.

---

43. Translator: The Alaca Çay valley.

The Church of St. Krikor Apughamrents, built 1040.

This small church, which can only hold about forty to sixty people, has three beautiful doors.[44] In some places, the polished stones have fallen and seem likely to have been destroyed. The following inscription can be read on the external northern wall.

In the year 489 (1040), I Aplgharip, Marzpan of the Armenians, son of Grigor and grandson of Apughamir, of the Armenian princes, although I was neglected by my father because I was the younger [child], I was nonetheless compelled by filial love for my parents, and I built this place of rest for my father Krikor and my brother Hamze and my sister Seda[45] and built two chapels for Saint Stepanos and St. Krikor . . . the terms for the priests are these: that every Friday they enter the Holy of Holies and perform a religious service for my mother Shushan, and Saturday for my father Krikor,

---

44. Translator: This must be a mistake; perhaps the author meant four to six people? The main space of the church measures only about 6 meters in diameter.

45. Translator: Orbeli transcribes this word as [. . . ɨ imo seda]—most likely, given the context, "my sister Seda."

and in St. Kristapawr every Friday for my [maternal] uncle Sago and Saturday for my brother Hamze, and instead of the Friday of [the Fast of] the Catechumens[46] and *aghuhatsit* Friday,[47] they will celebrate it on the eight free days.[48] Now, if any of the priests of those churches obstruct that service or become lazy and let days pass, let him be anathematized by the Father, Son and the Holy Spirit and by the 318 patriarchs, and let his lot be with Judas and Satan; may he who carries out this writing be blessed, amen.[49]

Kakgashen Church of St. Krikor [St. Gregory]

In the year 1000, King Kakig I built the marvelous Kakgashen Church of St. Krikor a short distance from the banks of the Dzaghadzor, fairly close to the palace of the Pakradunis. It is unique due to its extraordinary architectural style, which is similar to the famous Zvartnots Church near Holy Etchmiadzin. Professor Marr recently discovered this church, which draws any learned visitor to notice its unusual architecture. The churches that we have described up until now have either been quadrangular or polygonal. The St. Krikor Church, however, with four large arches forms a cruciform circle, and architectural historians have been astonished at its exceptional style and structure. This Kakgashen Church is also unusual because unlike the more typical construction of the main altar in front of the eastern wall, this church's main altar is in the center, that is, right in the center of the circle, so that one must climb it by stone steps. It is even more unusual because this church has three stories, and although it is in ruins down to its foundations, one can still see fragments of its original form. The gradually eroding two upper stories of the church stand on four huge columns

---

46. Translator: *Aṙajavorats* is the first fast or Lent of the Armenian Church, set by St. Krikor the Illuminator to start ten weeks before Easter. Friday is the last of its five days.

47. Translator: *Aghuhats* means literally "salt and bread," and here refers to the Fridays of fasting of Great Lent.

48. Translator: Meaning, free of fasting.

49. Translator: For an alternate reading, see Orbeli, 33.

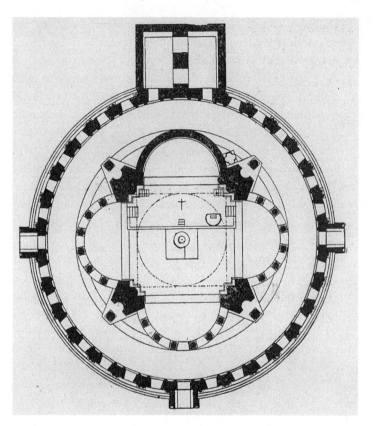

Floor plan of the Church of Zvartnots.

made of massive stones whose four carved capitals are eagles with spread wings. The bema of the main altar is approximately one and a half meters high and has three doors.

It is worth noting that the architectural style of the oldest churches, such as Zvartnots and this Kakgashen Church of St. Krikor, is totally unique. It is circular, tower-like, and as it gradually rises, it narrows. The main altar is exactly in the center of the circle, and is more elevated than is ordinary. Its bema rises with graduated square stepping stones.

The Kakgashen Church of St. Krikor was modeled on the architectural style of Zvartnots, as Asoghik has noted.[50]

Along the northern wall of this church, a stone statue of King Kakig I was excavated. The statue is larger than life, and in its stretched-out hands, there is an undamaged, miniature stone model of the church. For this reason, it has been easy to ascertain the original architectural style of this ruined church. It is a three-story tower ornamented with numerous windows and carvings which bear the mark of special care, and it is now in a glass case at the museum of Ani.[51] The statue of Kakig shows him in a long kaftan with wide sleeves, a wide turban on his head and a tassel hanging from each ear; he has an impressive face with a long beard, and a cross hanging from his chest.

Kakig's long robe and turban stirred the amazement of many because, as a Christian Armenian king, he had no occasion or need to wear the headdress characteristic of Muslims. We find the explanation of this in historical works, in which it is noted that the emirs of Baghdad would send to the Armenian Pakraduni kings, when they were ascending to the throne, turbans and robes characteristic of Muslim sovereigns as a royal emblem in place of a crown and staff. As the excavations of this church have only recently commenced, it is probable that new discoveries will soon be uncovered.

The Georgian Church

The Georgian Church was built a stone's throw from the Kakgashen Church of St. Krikor. Only one of its walls remains standing today.

---

50. See Chamchian's *History*, 873. [Translator: For this reference, see now *The Universal History of Stepanos Taroneci,* intr., trans., and comm. Tim Greenwood (Oxford: Oxford University Press, 2017), 312–313.]

51. Translator: "Three-story tower" (Balakian's *eṙayark ashdaragi*). This is exceptionally important and thus far neglected testimony to the three-tiered form of the model—with important implications for discussions of both the elevations of Kagkashen and Zvartnots, both long in ruins.

The interior of the Georgian Church.

The Georgians, who occupied Ani often during the eleventh and twelfth centuries, must have built this church during one of those periods. It is a small church built of polished stones in a quadrangular form. As depicted in the picture, its interior, with pillars and arches, is a beautiful construction. There are also several subterranean arches visible, and perhaps at one time these served as the church treasury. It is unfortunate that no traces of an inscription have been found thus far, but some are referring to this space as *nshkharadun*.[52]

The Palace of the Pakradunis

The Palace of the Pakradunis, which some call the Barracks, is built on the summit of Dzaghadzor at the most distant northwestern corner of Ani. It is a three-story edifice, built of polished stones, whose foundation on the side of the valley was built in part on thick, arcaded pillars and in part on a rampart. Its openings for light are as large as contemporary windows and it is worth noting that among

---

52. Translator: In Armenian, a place for making consecrated bread.

The façade of the Palace of the Pakradunis.

Southern view of the Palace of the Pakradunis.

all these ruins, there are no other buildings with such large windows except for the cathedral. It has an amazing door and is ornamented with carvings built in the Arabian architectural style on the eastern side, which is adorned with light red and black stones in a colorful mosaic.[53] Unfortunately it does not bear any inscription, or, more exactly, the stones bearing an inscription have fallen, because, in ancient times even an ordinary building would not have been left without an inscription, especially not a palace.

This ruined palace is the first building at Ani to have three-stories. For the most part, in earlier constructions, multiple-story buildings, and even two-story ones, were rare, and most had only one floor. If one looks from the western side of this palace downward, a wonderful panorama is revealed which makes a profound impression on one, especially with the deep valley's precipice, because from it, it is possible to see Dzaghadzor in all its breadth and length, and the Alaja [Alaca] Stream, which flows in a serpentine way into the Akhurian [Arpa] River near the Aghchegay Pert [Girls' Fortress]. It is also amazing to look down at the numerous caves and caverns dug into the flanks of Dzaghadzor. Some of them are natural and some have been dug out and are connected to each other through secret passages.

Unfortunately, even though Ani was a prominent capital city, there are no traces of palaces except for this one, other than the ruins of the Bahlavuni Palace in the Citadel. However, the remains of numerous palaces and mansions of those life-loving Pakraduni kings should have been discovered by now, and so one can only conclude that greedy enemies plundered and destroyed them ages ago.

Ani's Residence of the Catholicos

The Residence of the Catholicos (now a museum), which is defined by its columns and arcades, is built on a rock on the road to the

---

53. Translator: Based on Balakian's use of "Arabian" to describe the gavit of the Holy Apostles church, we may assume that he refers here to the palace's Islamic appearance.

Ani's Residence of the Catholicos (14 by 12 meters), now a museum.

Citadel, and looks over Dzaghadzor's shores to the edge of the Akhurian valley. It was converted to a mosque during the era of the Seljuk conquest, and a huge hexagonal tower-minaret—a polygonal tower with polished stones—more than 20 meters high, with Arabic inscriptions, rises alongside the Residence of the Catholicos. It hasn't been ruined until now, and so it is easy to conclude how solidly it was built. Although it has not been possible to ascertain this from the inscription, from which only the word *Allah* can be read in Arabic, it is believed that the building had been the residence of the Catholicos, or a tribunal under which four arcaded cellar rooms were built and are still visible. It is referred to as a watchtower, a tribunal, or a mosque, and on the postcards of Ani, simply as "Ani's tower."

The Catholicos's residence is sometimes thought of as the royal assembly, and people are sometimes confused by its various names and often believe that these are the ruins of different buildings. But, the truth is, it is one building that has accrued different names during different periods and has served different purposes according to need. It is a single-story construction, 12 meters wide and 14 meters long, adorned with carvings and polished stones and built on the precipice of the Akhurian River. As its interior is arcaded and columniated, there is nothing else like it now at Ani. And perhaps we can only find its likeness in Ghoshavank as the royal assembly.[54]

As one can see in the photograph, the interior is very impressive and majestic thanks to its five- (at one time six-) columned and arcaded structure.[55] The thickness of the columns is 85 centimeters, and the capitals are adorned with carvings. The arches are half-egg-shaped and solid, so that despite the destructive effect of the centuries, they remain standing. There are five huge windows on the eastern wall (similar to the large windows of the cathedral) which looks toward the Akhurian valley. And through the windows you can see the Akhurian River, which like a big boa winds its way down the valley, sometimes running quietly and sometimes thunderously.

It is this building which Professor Nicholas Marr [Nikolai Yakovlevich Marr, 1865–1934] has recently converted into a museum by renovating the ruined parts and reinforcing it with two iron doors. So now, the old Residence of the Catholicos is called the Marr Museum of Ani. Upon entering the museum, we find open drawers of wood, one span wide and built on the facing wall on which there have been placed various examples of fine stone carvings found in the ruins of Ani. And, under the wall near the door, in closed glass cases, there are objects on display that were found during the excavations. Among these objects are parts of skeletons, pieces of leather; silk shirts removed from the princely tomb, with delicate embroidery often of animal shapes and in perfect condition; there are bows and over a hundred large and small arrow tips or darts made of iron; iron and stone axes; various tools; copper censers; tips of lances; delicate silk and iron ornaments; and there are also beautiful porcelain vessels, vases and plates, as well as fragments of iron

---

54. Translator: By "royal assembly" Balakian refers here to the *zhamatoun* of Ghoshavank (Horomos), famous for its massive columnar interior space.

55. Translator: The photograph does not show the interior of the museum.

chains, copper plates, iron locks, ancient iron door hinges, iron bolts, iron tables and porcelain vessels and glass lamps. A large many-branched candelabra is particularly worthy of notice. It is very rare and of great value.[56]

There are also many examples of many types of tools, vessels, carvings, guns, shields and many other items in these glass cases from which it is easy to ascertain the great strides in progress our ancestors achieved in the civilization of their time. The statue of Kakig I Pakraduni which was found in 1906 in the Kagkashen Church of St. Krikor is in a special glass showcase in this museum, and it remains a beautiful example of Armenian art of the tenth century. As we can see in the photograph, his Holiness the Catholicos was photographed next to it. Near this statute, there is a miniature model of the St. Krikor Church which was found undamaged and is now placed high up on the wall. It is a fine piece of work and thus appears to be the work of an accomplished artist. Professor Nicholas Marr has named the museum after himself and so it is called the Marr Museum, and every day it seems it is enriched with newly discovered items from the excavations.

A little further away there is another museum near Dzaghadzor which is a new building and is also used as a workshop for Professor Marr and his assistants. On top of it flies the Russian flag. The museum also has pieces of rock bearing Assyrian cuneiform inscriptions, as well as many large and small fragments of rock with Latin, Greek, Armenian, Arabic, and Georgian inscriptions; here, as well, there are also Armenian carved stone crosses [khachkars]. Among other things they are objects of great scholarly value, and by studying them it should be possible to determine many things and to learn more deeply the history of the civilization of the Armenians from the eighth to thirteenth centuries.

---

56. Translator: The candelabra is now located in the History Museum of Armenia, inv. no. 123-1325, 1328.

King Kakig (Gagik) I and Catholicos Matteos II of All Armenians.

Ani's Citadel

The once famous Citadel of Ani (960) is one of the most prominent ruins of the city. Ashod III the Merciful, the Pakraduni king, had it built shortly after assuming the throne. This solid citadel in its time awoke fear and terror among even the most formidable of the enemies who came to attack and pillage Ani. The citadel is built on the southernmost end of the promontory of Ani on a hill about 120 meters above the Akhurian River. As this is the only height in Ani, it dominates the entire city. As the fortress has been sufficiently cleared by Professor Marr the old divisions have been distinctly revealed, although it is difficult to definitively determine what

The famous Citadel.

Ruins of the Palace of the Bahlavuni inside the Citadel.

Girls' Fortress, on the historical cliff below; and chapel of the Citadel.

purpose or need those divisions served in ancient times, especially because inscriptions elucidating this have not yet been found.

The visitor today only finds the foundations of the ramparts that were built of monolithic stones of three to four *ganguns* [1.6 meters] and also the huge gates, crumbling arches, half-ruined stone domes, traces of secret passageways, and the massive remains of arches and domes scattered around. This is all that remains of Ani's famous Citadel.

It is thought that the Palace of the Bahlavunis was inside the citadel in which there certainly would have been the special apartments of the king and the princes, since we know from history that when the enemy besieged Ani, sometimes for months, the king and his entourage would withdraw to the Citadel for safety, as it was also connected to the Akhurian valley and river via secret passages for the purpose of getting water and other necessities.

A little below the Citadel on the promontory one finds the traces of two small chapels, the dome of one still partly standing, although they do not have any notable architectural features. As the hill of

The ruins of the bridge and the Bekhents Monastery on the Akhurian River.

The tomb of the royal princes in the Citadel.

the Citadel is the highest point of Ani, when a visitor looks down from the fortress at the Aghchegay Pert and the valley in the distance, where the Akhurian forms a great inner arc and flows south, he is overwhelmed with awe. There man's art and craft joined to nature's impregnable precipice made the Citadel so invulnerable that even the most powerful enemy would be forced to think more about his defeat than victory.

At the confluence of the Alaja [Alaca] stream and the Akhurian River at the most distant corner of Ani's promontory, with the Aghchegay Pert (Ghêz-Ghala), which is built on top of wedge-shaped bare cliffs, there is a chapel that can only be seen from the top of the Citadel. This reminds one of the fortifications the Genovese built along the Black Sea at impregnable places. In this spot, nature is wonderful in an inexplicable way, as is one's sense of excitement. It is impossible to stand here looking out at it all and fully take in this extraordinary landscape and scene. The huge ruins of the famous bridge over the Akhurian, which was two-storied and joined the two banks with an immense arch, is also visible as you look toward the cathedral.

One marvels at the great skill of art and craft of these medieval architects when one imagines this two-story bridge arching 30 meters above the water of the river on the colossal tear of the unfathomable valley.[57] Its immense arch, which had no columns, connected the two great tower-like bases built on each bank. Furthermore, when one realizes that this spot of the Akhurian River is 20 meters deep, perhaps more from the surface of the water to the elevation of the arch, and one is even more amazed because in that period they didn't know how to fit the joints of buildings with iron, one is even more amazed.

A short distance from the opposite bank of the bridge, there is a cemetery, where the citizens of the city were buried, but the tombs of the princes and aristocrats were in the city, just as the ruins of

---

57. Translator: Balakian is incorrect here; the bridge was only a one story structure.

The ruins of the royal bath.

the tombs of the royal princes were in the Citadel. The remaining
ruins of the Kusanats Monastery, or Monastery of the Virgins, are
visible near the bridge, just a short distance from the cathedral.
Some think that the monastery was dedicated to St. Stepanos. There
is also a small beautifully built chapel, with a columnated small
dome, called Bekhents Monastery that still remains standing.[58] On
the wall on the eastern side of this Monastery of the Virgins is the
following inscription.

> In the year 459 (1010), I Mate, chief of the secretaries of the
> *atabek*'s *amirspasalar* Shahnshah, and my spouse Teni and my
> brother Markos, we have, for the long life of patron Shahnshah,
> of Khuandze and of their son Zakare, and for the salvation of
> our spirits, brought water [to the monastery] and ensured its
> maintenance. In fact, when the baron had the goodness to give
> us this convent, or formerly the pious Tigran had brought

---

58. Translator: The Monastery of the Virgins is sometimes referred to as the
Bekhents Monastery.

The royal road which leads to the Akhurian River.

the water, the latter had changed course as a result of the abandonment.[59]

As the inscription reveals, this monastery was in ruins, and the individual, whose name is nearly illegible, brought water and had the monastery repaired.

Recently Professor Marr found one of Ani's markets, which is in a narrow street with small stone stalls facing one another. Toward the east from the Church of the Holy Savior we find the ruins of a royal bath which was built on top of the easternmost point of the ramparts at the edge of the Akhurian valley. There is a street also to be found on the path to the Citadel, from under which pipes made of baked earth have been removed. At one time these apparently brought water from the Alaja mountains to the city. The illustration above shows the royal arcaded road which goes to the river, begins near the royal baths, and then descends toward the valley and the

59. Translator: For a different version, see Orbeli, 63–64. There the inscription is said to be at the Church of Tigran Honents and the date is given as 759 (1310).

river. While the excavations continue, new discoveries always appear which continue to enrich the Marr Museum and also shed light on this earlier period of Armenian civilization.

Ghoshavank near Ani

Leaving the external walls of Ani and traveling about a quarter of an hour, one can see from the distance the Church of the Shepherd. A little further away, two triumphal towers appear which seem to have performed the function of a gate at one time. Ghoshavank (985) [the Monastery of Horomos], which means the "Pair Monastery," was built on a hill another quarter hour distant from these towers, or half an hour from Ani. It was given the name Monastery of Horomos because the monks had come from Greece.[60]

Stepanos Asoghik related that during the century of iconoclasm, Armenian priests fleeing from the Greeks under the leadership of Hovhannes Vardapet came to this village and built this famous monastery in 985, during the reign of King Abas.[61] Architects speak of the monastery with great admiration. It is fair to say that that the interior and especially the columniated forecourt or outer hall and the [inner] hall surpass any of the other the ruins at Ani.

This monastery of Horomos or Ghoshavank was built in the village of the same name, where the families of more than a hundred Armenian villagers live. The village is at the edge of the valley where the Akhurian River flows toward Ani. Horomos was built with such great architectural skill that, despite its being one of Ani's oldest structures, it has remained completely intact, and its magnificent dome dominates the surrounding hills. It was renovated in 1653 by a monk named Taniel of Dikranagerd. Aside from the dome, which

---

60. See Chamchian, *History*, vol. 2, p. 823.

61. Translator: The tradition of deriving the name Horomos from refugee Byzantine monks fleeing the empire is not from Stepanos but from the thirteenth-century Armenian writers, beginning with Kirakos Gandzaketsi. See Karen Matevosyan, "History of the Monastery of Horomos," in *Horomos Monastery: Art and History*, ed. Edda Vardanyan (Paris: Centre d'histoire et civilization, 2015), 21.

An external view of Ghoshavank (Monastery of Horomos) near Ani (16 by 10 meters).

is adorned with carvings, it has a beautiful columniated belfry, also adorned with carvings on which the image of Mary Mother of God was carved together with the following inscription in the lion and bull.

In 487 (1038) of the Armenian era, I Hovhannes Shahnshah, son of Gagik Shahnshah, gave my orchard which was in Koghb to my church St. Hovhannes which I built in the monastery of Horomos with this meeting hall [*zhamatun*], and one hundred loads of salt every year free of all misfortune in the period of the patriarchate of Lord Petros and the prelature of this congregation of Father Hovhannes. Now if anyone hereafter opposes this writing of mine and my donations, may he be responsible for my sins in front of God and be anathematized in his life and at his death by the 318 patriarchs in Nicaea, while those who keep firmly the inscription of my gifts be blessed by Christ.[62]

---

62. Translator: For a transcription and alternate translation of this inscription see Samvel Karapetyan and Jean-Pierre Mahé, "The Hoṙomos Inscriptions,"

On the inner and outer walls one can also see the inscription of the donation of this orchard, and numerous other inscriptions of this type which have remained unaltered due to the very solid condition of the construction.

On the arch to the left of the rear column of the belfry is found the following inscription.

These are the downtown real estates of this monastery of Horomos. Georg, the old priest, gave to this monastery his patrimonial houses close to the Gars Gate, in front of Surb-Stepanos, as well as other incomes: 3 masses the day of this feast. The cenobite Giwtik gave his patrimonial house on the cliff, and he received 3 masses (during the feast) of Khachgyud.[63]

Similarly, opposite the western door of the belfry is the following inscription.

(1229). By the grace of Christ, I, Vasak, son of Davit—who was the grandson of king Kiwrike—, lord of Norberd, confessor of Christ, became affiliated to this holy congregation and gave to Surb-Yovanes, [as a] present, the oil-press which I had bought from this monastery, paying cash and with all confirmation. Under the prelacy of Ter Barsegh, son of Amir Erkat, and in exchange, they rewarded me with celebrating mass every year, during the feast of the Holy Vardanank, in all of the churches: as long as I am alive, they will do it for Varham and Tamar, and after my decease, for me. Now those who perform this writing, will be blessed by Christ, and [if anyone] opposes it, he will be separated and will inherit the curses of Cain, Judas, and the Antichrist, whoever he is, and may there be no remission for ever! Amen.[64]

---

in *Horomos Monastery: Art and History*, ed. Edda Vardanyan (Paris: Centre d'histoire et civilization, 2015), 417–418.

63. Translator: This translation is from *Horomos Monastery: Art and History*, ed. Edda Vardanyan (Paris: Centre d'histoire et civilization, 2015), 457.

64. Translator: For this translation and a transcription, see *Horomos Monastery: Art and History*, ed. Edda Vardanyan (Paris: Centre d'histoire et civilization, 2015), 446–447.

It is understood from these inscriptions that a person named Vasak grandson of King Kiwrige and son of Davit donated an olive press to this church, which appears to have been at one time dedicated to St. Hovhannes, since it is mentioned thus in other inscriptions. He lays down the condition that a special mass be conducted for his soul on the day of the feast of Holy Vardanants.

On the eastern arch of the belfry the following inscription can be read.

In the year 677 (1228) by the will of the almighty God, this is our memorial writ (of me) the *hechup* Grigor, son of Hasan, and my nephews, with me, Ishkhan, son of Kurd, and my nephews, (since we are) lords over this holy congregation, the monastery of Horomos. We have decreed, by (this) inscription, that [if] any patron of this place, whoever he may be, either a man or a woman, lets himself be bribed to install the abbot, such [a person] should receive the anathema of Judas, who has sold God, and that of Cain, who has killed his brother. In addition, may the abbot, along with the other administrators who will offer a bribe, openly or in secret, be cursed, soul and body, by the heavenly Father, the 318 patriarchs and all the saints. May the abbot who will sell part of the livelihood of this monastery or embezzle part of the [belongings] of this monastery be anathematized in life and in death! Whoever of the patrons or of the members of the congregation will oppose this word, or will try to erase this writ, may he also be erased from the Book of Life! May those who perform it be blessed by God! Amen.[65]

In this inscription, giving bribes or embezzling the income of the monastery is prohibited through anathema.

There exists also the following inscription on the edge of the arch of the third column.

By the grace of God, I, Lord Grigor son of Apughamr, archbishop of the metropolis of Ani, gave to St. Yovanes, [as a] present, the

---

65. Translator: For this translation and a transcription, see *Horomos Monastery: Art and History*, ed. Edda Vardanyan (Paris: Centre d'histoire et civilization, 2015), 444–445.

The arcaded and columniated interior part of the royal assembly hall in Ghoshavank.

pastoral income of the villages of Akank, Shawta, and Aghbnagegh, under the prelacy of Andreas *vardapet*, who loves sanctity. And the [priests] in charge of this [church] will celebrate every year 2 masses. . . . May whoever keeps [this] firmly be blessed by God. Amen.[66]

There are also numerous inscriptions of this type on the walls of the sanctuary and the pillars and arches of the belfry which I'm not even mentioning because the meaning of each one is the same: that is, by giving a donation to the church, the donor has set a day for a mass for his soul. He promises for whoever fulfills his request, the blessing of God, while those who disrespect his memory will receive the curse of Cain and Judas.

This church with its columniated and arcaded interior parts and forecourts makes a profound impression on the pilgrim. It now has

---

66. Translator: For this translation and a transcription, see *Hoṙomos Monastery: Art and History*, ed. Edda Vardanyan (Paris: Centre d'histoire et civilization, 2015), 442.

The chapels of St. Minas and St. Kevork in the valley of Ghoshavank.

an abbot, and religious services are being conducted. Next to this famous sanctuary there is a great hall built with huge stones, and it is columniated with carved arches and capitals and resembles the interior of Ani's Residence of the Catholicos (now the museum). At one time this great interior was a meeting hall for the king and feudal lords, and even now the place for the royal throne is clearly visible.

The Akhurian River can be seen from the heights of the hill of Ghoshavank, slithering and flowing toward Ani. It passes by a hot spring, which because of its sulphurous water, is a place that is popular with the sick who come here hoping to be cured. There are also two chapels in this valley, St. Minas and St. Kevork, whose domes, until recently, were standing. However, due to negligence of a minor repair, they are now ruined. There are also various inscriptions on these two chapels, but it is very difficult to read them. Next to the St. Kevork one finds the tomb of Ashod III the Merciful, one of the famous Pakraduni kings. There is a large stone on top of a pedestal of two stone steps on which is written "Ashod the Merciful." Eyewitnesses relate that until recently there was also a chapel on this

The tomb of King Ashod the Merciful near the aforementioned
St. Kevork chapel.

royal grave which was similarly destroyed because of the lack of
renovation. As the old inscription of Ashod the Merciful is not leg-
ible, the priest of the village had a new one written, without understanding that touching this kind of relic of antiquity is really a
sacrilege.

The current state of this tomb of this famous Armenian king of
the Pakradunis is simply pitiful. The grave of this good and virtuous king today is just a piece of inglorious rock (see the picture), and
that king, who in his time had pity for everyone, today is in need
of compassion. Is there no wealthy Armenian who can repair his
grave and adorn it—a grave which, although speechless, issues a
silent reproach to every humane and caring Armenian who visits it.

It is impossible to see the extent of these ruins of Ani and not
be touched or not to weep. How could the Armenian visitor not be
moved and not shed tears, especially when he recalls that there was
a time when this city was full of a commotion and vitality that was
a part of this great city, where there are now only dilapidated royal
palaces, half-ruined but magnificent churches, and collapsed barracks inside the old solid ramparts; and that at one time, Armenian

princes, feudal lords, and martial Bahlavuni *sparapet*s [military commanders] lived here and won fame. It was here that our holy ancestors lived, prayed, and were massacred by enemies who attacked Ani from all directions, and in part because Armenians were preserving their nationality and their Christian faith brought to them by the Holy Illuminator.

Truly it is an impossible thing to recall all this and not be moved, since every stone cross and inch of soil is inundated and irrigated with the blood and tears of the Armenians; every ruin and every inscription, and every column or arch ornamented with carvings has an ancient story of its past glory.

CHAPTER IV

Scholarship on Ani

Part I: The Armenian Architectural Style

Armenian and European scholars consider Ani to be a great museum of various architectural styles and also a display of the arts and crafts of Armenian artists and artisans of this period. The European scholarly travelers who have visited Ani have been impressed by the unique Armenian style of architecture, and have gathered new knowledge about the art and crafts of the Middle Ages which didn't exist in Europe.

While the medieval cities of Europe have been dramatically changed and their buildings transformed by the evolution of daily life and history, Ani remains unchanged and in its original state. From the time of its final destruction in 1348, Ani ceased to be a living city, and soon became a pile of ruins. Since then, there have been no inhabitants either inside the city or in its environs except for in a few small villages.

The magnificent architectural construction of Ani's ruins, and the rich variety of carvings suggest that during that creative period of the Pakraduni kings, Armenian art and crafts began to reach the height of its development. Thus, in many ways we can call the period of rule of the Pakradunis (the tenth to eleventh centuries) an Armenian golden age. It is also worth noting that although we have ruins remaining from old capitals of the pre-Christian era of the Armenians in the Ararat plain and its environs, they have not been the subject of any special study, so that it is difficult to characterize at present the Armenian architectural style of the pre-Christian era. Some, however, think that Persian and Armenian architecture bear a similar origin, and some believe that they have drawn inspiration from each other. Those European specialists argue that the Armenians, because they became Christian and often were oppressed by the Persians, turned toward the West, toward Europe, for inspiration for their crafts, art, and, in general, civilization, so that by entering into contact with Christian Europe, Armenians gradually seasoned their art with some European styles. In the period of Arab domination, Armenian art also underwent some Arabic influence.

Some wish to defend this hypothesis by arguing that, as in Persian and Arabic art, in the Armenian architectural style the presence of living beings is lacking. In other words, the art of sculpture is not found in the ruins of Ani. Also, in seeing a similarity in the carvings, some scholars hypothesize that there is a Persian and Arabic influence, and think that the similarities of columns and the forms of domes also show that there is some borrowing from the basic forms of Romanesque and Gothic and also a little bit from Norman architectural styles. Some scholars also see the low arches of windows and doors as an imitation of the Byzantine style.

Finally, in the opinion of other scholars, the art of Armenian architecture is the continuation of different architectural styles which bear the influence of different historical eras. Such scholars argue that Armenian architecture has undergone the influence of Roman, Byzantine, Gothic, Persian, and Arabic architecture. Yet there are also European scholars who see, in the Armenian architectural style, creativity more than imitation. From this perspective, I would quote the opinion of several European scholars who after visiting Ani have published extensive studies celebrating the Armenian genius and expressing their admiration.

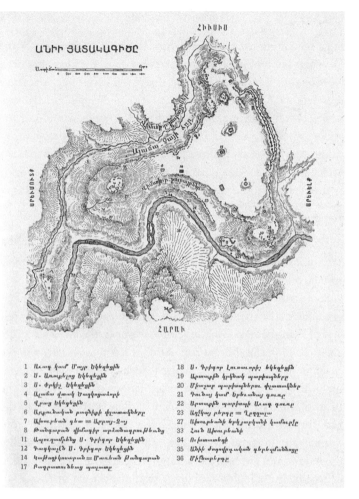

ԱՆԻԻ ՅԱՏԱԿԱԳԻԾԸ

ՀԻՒՍԻՍ

ԱՐԵՒՄՈՒՏՔ

ԱՐԵՒԵԼՔ

ՀԱՐԱՒ

Plan of Ani Key: 1. Cathedral; 2. Church of the Holy Apostles; 3. Church of the Holy Savior (Surp Prkitch Church); 4. Alaja Stream of Dzaghatzor; 5. Georgian Church; 6. Ruins of the royal bath; 7. Akhurian River (Arpa Chay); 8. Museum of Stone Inscriptions; 11. Apughamrents Church of St. Krikor; 12. Kakgashen Church of St. Krikor; 14. Residence of the Catholicos (Marr Museum of Ani); 17. Palace of the Pakradunis; 18. St. Krikor the Illuminator Church; 19. External double walls; 20. Ruins of the single-line walls; 21. Dvin (Yerevan Gate); 22. Main gate of the external wall; 23. Girls' Fortress; 27. Bridge of the Akhurian River; 33. The passage of the Akhurian River; 34. Place of pilgrimage; 35. Ani's common cemetery; 36. The citadel.

His Holiness Matteos II Izmerlian, Catholicos of All Armenians.

Among the European voyagers who have visited Ani, the English traveler H. F. B. Lynch, the author of *Armenia: Travels and Studies* (London, 1901), writes about both the old and new cities of Armenia (and has numerous color plates). About Ani's cathedral he notes, "The interior [. . .] has many of the characteristics of the Gothic

style, of which it establishes the Oriental origin."[67] Lynch wishes to
say by this that Armenian architecture did not receive the Gothic
style from Europe; on the contrary, Europe obtained the Gothic style
from the Orient, of course in its primitive form, which over time the
Europeans developed and advanced. This thesis is also supported by
the fact that the origin of Gothic architecture belongs to the Middle
Ages. In other words, the style of Gothic architecture began to
develop in the tenth century, which coincides almost with the end of
the Pakraduni period, when in Ani, Armenian architecture had
already begun to reach the stage of its highest development. It is also
at the end of the tenth century when the cathedral of Ani was built at ·
the hands of the famous Armenian architect Drtad.

While Lynch ascribes the origin of Gothic architecture to the
East, another scholar, the Frenchman [Charles] Texier goes a step
further with a definite assertion that the Gothic style has an Armenian origin, and that the architectural chef d'oeuvre style, Gothic,
had come to central Europe by means of emigration from the city
of Arpa Chay, which is another name for Ani and the Turkish name
of the Akhurian River.[68]

Thus, when the first invasions of Ani by Alpaslan began in 1064,
some of the population began to migrate in groups to Poland, Wal-
lachia, Moldavia, and central Europe, and they brought with them,
among other things, their arts and crafts. Thus the Armenians of Ani
created a foundation in medieval central Europe for the incomparable Gothic style, which in its forms and variety of beautiful carving
and stonework was the chef d'oeuvre of all architectural styles.

I would note among those monumental achievements of Gothic
architecture: Venice's San Marco basilica, Milan's cathedral, Paris's
Notre Dame, and London's Westminster Abbey, each known to the
world as glorious expressions of Gothic architecture from their
respective historical moments. Thus, Ani's renowned cathedral bears

---

67. Translator: H. F. B. Lynch, *Armenia: Travels and Studies*, vol. 1 (London:
Longmans, Green, 1901), 372.
68. op. cit., 390.

the early imprint of Gothic architecture. Its tall and delicate columns, its ovoid interior, and its hollow arches have inspired marvel in European scholarly travelers.[69] Lynch observes, as well, that the roof is more Byzantine and built with less delicacy of architectural art.

Lynch also praises with great enthusiasm the talent Armenians have had in the arts and crafts, stressing in particular their native genius in architecture. Historically it is not difficult to document and establish the singular talent Armenians have had in the art and technology of architecture. For example, the tenth-century Armenian historian Stepanos Asoghik of Taron [Moush], who wrote the contemporary history of the Pakraduni kings, explained much about the construction and flourishing of Ani, noted that Drtad, who built the cathedral of Ani, was a renowned architect who was called to Constantinople to renovate Hagia Sophia—which I think everyone will agree is one of the wonders of the world and the chef d'oeuvre of Byzantine architecture. The fact that Drtad was chosen, among all the prominent Greek and European architects of this era, is a tribute to Armenian genius. It was Drtad who was entrusted with the formidable challenge of renovating the Hagia Sophia Church after it was damaged in a great earthquake in the tenth century.

In writing about the cathedral, Lynch goes on:

> The cathedral will surprise the traveller, even if he has come from Edgmiatsin . . . he will have the impression of a stately simplicity underlying the diversity of outline and form. . . . Although the interior is almost free of ornament, the art of the sculptor has been employed upon the enrichment of the outside niches, of the doorways and windows, and in the moldings of the false arcade. In no case do we discover any trace of barbarism; the designs are sober and full of grace; the execution is beyond praise. The impression which we take away from our survey of these many features is that we have been introduced to a monument of the highest artistic

---

69. Translator: Drtad's ingenious technique of creating hollowed arches for structural support during earthquakes was also an admired innovation.

merit, denoting a standard of culture which was far in advance of the contemporary standards in the West.[70]

It is significant, I think, that an English intellectual should value Armenian genius and ancient Armenian architecture so highly.[71] It seems to me that no matter how indifferent or uninformed a person might be about the fine points of architectural art, he will be deeply impressed when he stands inside the Cathedral and gazes at the magnificent arches above him, the fine and huge pillars characteristic of the Gothic style, the capitals adorned with carvings and various other features.

If we wish to summarize the chief characteristics of the Armenian architectural style of the buildings of Ani, we can say the following: (1) General simplicity of the style of the architectural plan; (2) Integrity, and in various parts perfect harmony of the architectural structure; (3) In order to avoid monotony, abundance of arches, pillars, and carvings and particular regularity in ornamentation, without boastful superfluity; (4) Decorum and rich variety of carved ornamentation; (5) A mysterious darkness that is observable in this type of ancient Armenian construction, which is neither darkness nor light, and which leaves the viewer with a mystical feeling or experience. This corresponds with the church's aim of nourishing the soul; (6) The pointed cupola positioned in the middle of Armenian temples is also a native characteristic of Armenian architecture; no other Christian church has this feature, and we find it, beginning with the cathedral of Holy Etchmiadzin, on the majority of old and new Armenian churches in the Caucasus.

Aside from these general traits, it is observable in particular that often columns are slender and tall, as in the Cathedral, while sometimes they are short and thick, as in the Residence of the Catholicos in Ani and Ghoshavank's royal or princely assembly hall. Similarly, capitals are sometimes adorned with carvings, as in the capitals of

---

70. Translator: Lynch, vol. 1, p. 368.

71. Translator: Lynch's maternal grandfather was Armenian.

the columns of St. Krikor the Illuminator, and sometimes plain, as in the Cathedral. Generally, the models for the carvings are taken from nature, and in turn represent trees, vines, flowers, and animals, but nowhere to be found are human images with which Byzantine architecture is so rich.

As we said at the beginning of our last chapter, when Armenian architecture was subject to Persian and Arabic influence there was no longer any sculpture of animate beings. When, however, Armenian architecture became more influenced by Byzantine and European styles, it gradually developed more images of living creatures and more colorful images. However, Armenian artisans and sculptors were always cautious about the reproduction of human beings. The only exception until now has been the statue of King Gagik I, which is not a terribly refined work.

Nonetheless it is undeniable that Armenian architecture is an art which developed independently in the heart of Armenia, though it was not exempt from historical evolution, and bore Persian, and later Arabic influence. For example, there is some Arabic influence on the external door of St. Krikor the Illuminator Church, which is built on a rock. Similarly, the great external gate of the Church of the Holy Apostles is a wonderful example of Arabic architecture, and so is the face of the main door of the Palace of the Pakradunis, which is made of a light red and black mosaic, which is ornamented. It is unfortunate that visitors have taken pieces of these stones for souvenirs, which has contributed to the destruction of this precious building. It is simply an act of vandalism and desecration.

The Church of St. Krikor the Illuminator was built in a harmonious coupling of Gothic and Byzantine styles, while the Kakgashen Church of St. Krikor represents an unparalleled architectural style, as it is based on the plan of the Zvartnots Church near Holy Etchmiadzin. As Stepanos Asoghik notes, the Zvartnots Church, which already had been destroyed when Kakig I constructed this Kakgashen St. Krikor Church, was made in memory of the marvelous architecture of Zvartnots.

As for the ancient art of Armenian masonry, the craft of early and medieval Armenian masonry is noteworthy because, while old and new constructions were built with polished stones on the exterior walls, at Ani, and more generally in the ancient and medieval ruins of the Ararat and Shirag plains, one finds polished stones on both the exterior and interior walls. Furthermore, the stones are joined with such care, and both external and interior walls are made with cleansed or polished stones which are joined with great refinement, and this has become a subject of great interest for scholars who have visited Ani.

The stones of the buildings of Ani are a type of volcanic rock particular to the Ararat plain, and in their native state are soft and easily polished. Because of this, the stones used in building are able to be worked and polished in a clean manner, like marble. While these volcanic stones are so soft and easy to polish and grind, with the passing of centuries they harden, so the buildings gradually become even more solid and firm and can endure the potential destruction of time. These volcanic stones also have the virtue of not being monochrome, as they are found in black, red, pink, and gray. If they are arranged creatively with aesthetic skill they are gorgeous, and can even evoke the idea of a mosaic.

It is noteworthy also that among these kinds of medieval buildings, multistory constructions are quite rare. At most they have two stories and only very rarely have three, as the Palace of the Pakradunis has. Generally the windows are narrow and tall, and only rarely are they wide, as in the windows of the Cathedral and the Palace of the Pakradunis; and rarely are windows round, as are several small and round windows on the outer walls of the St. Krikor the Illuminator Church. Like these narrow and tall windows, the small and low doors of these buildings are done in an early Gothic style.

In general, there are inscriptions on these buildings. Sometimes they are engraved on walls, or on doors, arches, or pillars. The history of the construction can be read in these inscriptions, for example: when the structure was built, whence it came, who the benefactors were, and so on. The writing is usually Mesropian, and easy to read for the adept.[72]

I can't overestimate the value of these ruins. They shed great light on Armenian history in the Middle Ages, on Armenian civilization, and on the character, and moral and intellectual state of the Armenian people at the time. Armenian historians have said very little about all this in their writings; rather, they have concentrated on writing about the wars that have besieged Armenia—both internal and external—and often in epic terms.

Part II: The Present Excavations of Ani

It is indeed grievous that a capital city of the Armenians as famous as Ani, being so close to Etchmiadzin and Tiflis, has remained abandoned until now. Our sorrow is further accentuated when we consider that the Throne of the Illuminator of the Patriarch of All Armenians is in Etchmiadzin, while Tiflis is the Caucasian center of Armenian millionaires. Aside from the passing Armenian and European traveler, until this time, no one has seriously studied the ruins of Ani. Until now not one scientific investigation or excavation has been conducted, although at various times Armenian, and more so European, scholars have visited and studied Ani, some of whom have published their travel notes and studies, and always with praise for the Armenian architectural genius. It is only now with these scientific excavations that we can evaluate the genuine aesthetic and artisanal value of Ani's ruins, and only now can we fully expose to the scholarly world the medieval civilization of the Armenians.

This initiative fell to Professor Nicholas Marr, and the Armenian people are forever grateful to this Armenologist, who brought such attention to the culture of Armenian art and architecture and helped place it in relation to Europe. Professor Marr is equally proud to have been the initiator of Ani's scientific excavations. He is English

---

72. Translator: Here Balakian refers to the classical Armenian alphabet invented by Mesrop Mashtots around 405.

on his father's side, Georgian on his mother's, and his wife is Russian; and he is also a member of Petersburg's Imperial Academy of Sciences, and has been a lecturer in Armenian in the philological branch of the Russian Imperial University of St. Petersburg. He began visiting Ani in 1893 and did some small-scale research there until 1904, when he began more in-depth scientific excavations. From that time on he took his summer vacations in Ani, and through great sacrifice began the process of cleaning up Ani's ruins and putting them in order. His greatest achievement, and his legacy, will be in creating Ani's Archaeological Museum, which bears his name. It is rich with objects and artifacts from the ruins, as I noted earlier.

Professor Nicholas Marr presented the scientific value of the ruins of Ani in special reports to the Petersburg's Imperial Archaeological Academy, and this awoke great interest in Ani in the scholarly world. Yet it is hard to believe that the Imperial Archaeological Academy of the Russian capital, with all of its resources, doesn't financially support Professor Marr at Ani except for a few hundred rubles yearly, which doesn't even cover the cost of traveling back and forth from Ani to Petersburg.

Petersburg's Armenian church council, however, does support Professor Marr with almost 3,000 rubles yearly for the expenses of the excavations. This support made the excavations possible and encouraged Marr to keep going. Yet, even though the Imperial Archaeological Academy of the Russian capital comes up with the bare minimal travel expenses for Marr, rumors reached us in Etchmiadzin that Petersburg is considering moving Marr's Ani Museum to Petersburg. I believe that Peterburg's Imperial Archaeological Academy will make a terrible mistake if it tries to move the museum there because the thousands of visitors from many nations who visit Ani now will never have the opportunity nor the means to visit the museum in Petersburg.

If the Academy is going to move the museum to Petersburg so it will be in the great Russian capital I would hope that both the Patriarch in Holy Etchmiadzin and Professor Marr himself will protest. It is appropriate and impressive for Ani's museum to be in Ani, and furthermore, the work of those conducting research is easier this way. Furthermore, the Russian government should not take artifacts out of Ani—because the artifacts are both a source of great pride and even consolation.[73]

Ani's Archaeological Museum is still not decorated and catalogued in a fully scientific way; it is waiting to be fully put together so Marr's superb work can be fully realized. Although he has presented yearly special reports on the Ani excavations for his scholarly contributions to the Imperial Academy of Archaeology of Petersburg, he will have made his greatest contribution to the Armenians when he publishes the scientific work of his excavations, which will demonstrate the brilliant medieval civilization of the Armenians in its different stages.

Although Eugène Boré, Hamilton, Texier, Brosset, and other European scholars have published both extensive and concise studies on ancient Armenian civilization, and in particular on Ani, we hope that Professor Marr's study of Ani's excavations will surpass all of them, because it will be based on numerous proofs and positive foundations. Professor Marr[74] also has three university students working with him, and they provide great assistance to this arduous labor.[75] The Armenian scholar Toros Toramanian[76] has been a

---

73. Translator: This discussion of these artifacts, and their planned move to Saint Petersburg, is further notable in light of their disappearance during the First World War and the Armenian Genocide.

74. We regret that we were unable to have extensive biographical information on Professor Marr.

75. We will not speak at further length on Prof. Marr's work concerning the Ani excavations since we already wrote at length about the essentials on this in our third chapter's descriptive section.

76. The architect Toramanian is from Turkey's Karahisar district and was born near the ruins. He is about fifty years old. He received his education at Constantinople's Imperial Fine Arts Academy. After the Armenian massacres [of the 1890s], having gone to Romania and made a good amount of money, he went to Paris in order to perfect his specialization, and upon Mr. G. Basmajian's invitation in 1902, they traveled together to Ani in 1902 for scientific investigations. From that time to the present he remains in Ani, working as a scholar unable to leave the great museum of medieval Armenian crafts and art.

colleague and an assistant to Professor Marr and the excavations in Ani. Despite his modesty, he has erudite knowledge of crafts and art, and is a noble person with a good heart and soul. He is so dedicated to studying the architecture of Ani that despite numerous financial and moral deprivations, he conducted detailed studies from 1902 on, under horrific conditions, and remained with the cheerful steadfastness of an obstinate scholar dedicated to his work. His goal is to verify the originality and achievements of the Armenian architectural style and Armenian arts and crafts of the Middle Ages. As a true and self-sustaining scholar, Toramanian is amazed at these remnants of medieval Armenian architecture which bear the imprint of native Armenian genius. Whether they are pieces of stone crosses, of carved columns, capitals, or arches, any remnant— this scholar studies and envisions with precision. Thus he has greatly aided the work of Professor Marr's excavations, and has enhanced the scholarly significance of the ruins.

Without Toramanian's professional assistance, Professor Marr's excavations would have been extremely difficult, if not impossible, because, though Professor Marr is an archaeologist and a scholar of European renown, he is not a specialist in the art and technology of architecture. And, without architectural erudition, it is impossible to ascertain the style and forms of the ruins at Ani and complete an understanding of the missing parts of the various ruins which have been unearthed.

Toramanian prepared 300 pictures and floor plans of all the ruins of Ani and Ghoshavank. He also drew 2,500 pictures of the arches, pillars, capitals, doors, and examples of carvings on other surfaces which depict the likeness of flowers, plants, and various animals, as well as decorative pieces carved on stone that are like lace. As I've already noted, nowhere do you encounter carvings in the likeness of men, something which our ancestors always avoided, while by contrast Byzantine architecture is rich in those representations.

All of Toramanian's work has been presented at Petersburg's Russian Imperial Academy with the help of Professor Marr's generous efforts. Toromanian's presentations there were received with high praise and he was also given a certificate of honor. We also owe to this erudite antiquity-loving architect the preparation of the floor plan of the church of Zvartnots near Holy Etchmiadzin, which he completed with scholarly precision, making inferences from certain fragments even if they are but a small, shattered piece of a wall, window, column, capital, or arch. As the plan of Zvartnots is the same as that of the Kakgashen Church of St. Krikor, I placed it in the descriptive section of this book in order to give the reader an idea about the style of ancient Armenian architecture.

Thanks to Toramanian's investigations and studies of Ani, Ghoshavank, Holy Etchmiadzin, and other churches in this region, it is now understood that Armenian architecture of the ninth to eleventh centuries is not a copy of Byzantine or any other architecture, but an independently fostered art. Still, there may be aspects of Byzantine, Persian, and Arabic styles which I have already noted at length.

It is unfortunate that Toramanian's studies, which were done through such privation, remain unpublished, and not one of our very rich magnates has yet become a patron of this esteemed architect in order to facilitate the publication of his important work. His work has been done with great precision, and the scholarly community would find his studies a significant contribution to shedding light on ancient Armenian civilization and Armenian medieval architecture.

Another young Armenian architect, a specialist in Armenian architecture, Arshag Fetvadjian, has traveled to hundreds of ruins in the vast Ararat plain and the district of Shirag. In this way, then, he joins Professor Marr and Toramanian in forming a trinity of complementary scholars who have brought the power of ancient Armenian civilization and architecture to light in the scholarly world.

Fetvadjian also has reached the conclusion that Armenian architecture is an independent style despite its various influences—which is true of all architectural styles—since no style can sprout like a mushroom from one day to the next, grow and progress, without bearing the influence of the climate, environment, neighboring nations, and the psychological influence of the people. Despite his youth, Fetvadjian is serious and dedicated. Having received his architectural education in France, he has traveled frequently to Italy, Egypt, Palestine, and Greece, and accumulated great erudition on the antiquities of these classical cultures, and, thanks to these studies, he has a wellspring of knowledge for the scholarly research he has conducted in the Armenian ruins. Many of us have had the opportunity to see the hundreds of paintings, plans, and other pictures which he always copied in situ, and they are serious and professional and need to be published immediately.

Fetvadjian has also discovered that the architectural style of ancient Armenian temples is also apparent in ancient Coptic churches, and that there are various similarities between the Armenian and Coptic styles. I am sure that an explanation for this will emerge from new research.

In a word, the archaeological and architectural studies of Professor Marr, Toramanian, and Fetvadjian on ancient Armenian arts and crafts are groundbreaking for contemporary scholarship, and will surely have an influence on the current state of architecture and art historical scholarship.

It is also pertinent to note that there is a monastery near the cathedral in Ani where a *vardapet* is always in residence with a servant. He is simultaneously abbot of Ani and Ghoshavank. This is the monastery in which pilgrims and visitors are given shelter. The abbot *vardapet* conducts religious services in the Cathedral and in the St. Krikor the Illuminator Church, and also performs mass on feast days as the pilgrims desire. He also keeps the keys to the Marr Museum, and he watches over all the old and new constructions and ruins of Ani. It would be good, of course, for the abbacy of Ani and Ghoshavank to be more organized and have more provisions for the reception and comfort of pilgrims.

His Holiness Catholicos Matteos II's Voyage to Ani

When the Holy Patriarch arrived in Petersburg and was presented to the Russian Tsar with exceptional honors, Professor Marr performed the office of translator between the Tsar and the

The official patriarchal group: His Holiness Catholicos Matteos
Izmerlian, G. Archbishop Sathunian, M. Bishop Der Movsesian, Yeprem
Vartabed, Bapken Vartabed, Khoren Vartabed, Mesrob Vartabed,
Balakian Vartabed, Oukhthanes Vartabed, Professor Nikolai Marr, Minas
Cheraz, Teacher Isahag Haroutiunian.

Catholicos, and he requested then that the Holy Patriarch be
allowed to visit Ani during his voyage from St. Petersburg to
Holy Etchmiadzin. His Holiness accepted this invitation with joy.

Of all the members of our patriarchal retinue, I think I was full of
the greatest joy, because our companions—the bishop and the other
vartabeds, had visited Ani on other occasions, and only I and my
one other vartabed colleague, as Turkish-Armenians, had not been
able to visit Ani. Although I had the opportunity, in October of
1908, as delegate for the Catholicosal elections, to travel to Holy
Etchmiadzin, and then go to Ani apropos of our visit to Alexandrapol, our train got buried in an intense blizzard so that traveling
to Ani was impossible. I remember how the packs of hungry wolves

were wandering around in the snow where we were stalled, and how this made it an even more forbidding moment.

Having lost that moment then, I was overjoyed with this opportunity to see Ani—I had such a thirst to see those eternal monuments of the past glory of our forefathers. I wanted to kiss that holy soil and the broken stone crosses and half-destroyed ruins which our ancestors made with their blood and tears. At Tiflis, after extraordinarily warm and popular receptions and ceremonies worthy of a king, the patriarchal train with its retinue, joined by the men and women of the Tiflis Organizing Committee, left the station. Stopping at the famous monastery of Sanahin, on June 24, 1909, and then after ten hours, we finally arrived at the only entirely Armenian city of the Shirag plain, Alexandropol, from which it was easier to travel to Ani.

Although I'm leaving out the details of the magnificent reception by the Armenian population there in honor of the newly elected Holy Patriarch, I think it is important to say some things about this city. Alexandrapol[77] is 1,320 meters above sea level and endures the severe winters of the fertile Shirag plain. Its old name was Gyumri, and in 1830 the famous Russian general Paskevich conquered the city from the Ottoman state. At that time Bishop Karapet of Karin (Erzurum)[78] led 90,000 Armenians to immigrate to the region, and many of them to Alexandrapol.

Now it has a population of 30,000, of which only 1,000 are Russian, Turkish, Greek, and Armenian Catholic. The remaining 29,000 are Armenian Apostolic (Orthodox), so that the administration of the city is in the hands of the latter. The Armenians have built wonderful churches in the architectural style of Ani's cathedral, a mayoral office building, as well as various national [Armenian] scholarly, literary, and artisanal societies. The people still speak with the Karin dialect, and are devout. It is hard to find such piety among the Armenian cities of the Caucasus or Russia. Alexandrapol is about ten hours from Tiflis and only three hours from Gars. It is

---

77. Translator: Present-day Gyumri.
78. Translator: Present-day Erzurum.

the central army headquarters for the Russian border guards because it is so near the Ottoman frontier. Thus there are always 20,000 soldiers ready for any eventuality in barracks near the city. Both city dwellers and villagers benefit from the commerce of so many soldiers. Without this commerce, the livelihood of the people would be much more difficult because, aside from growing grains, there are no other crops, nor is there a thriving community in the professions here, and so otherwise people live from hand to mouth.

The Poem of Ani

But let me return to our journey. After enjoying that enthusiastic reception in Alexandrapol, and a night of their warm hospitality, early on the morning of June 25 we set out for Ani as the scorching summer sun was rising from the side of Mt. Aragats. Our hearts and souls were full of joy and passion as we anticipated seeing Ani in just a few hours. Ani—which our forefathers built and made prosper. We would now be able to see those ruins which still emit and evoke those days of glory. Ani was the famous capital of the Pakraduni kings and a place of royal, aristocratic and princely wealth and ostentation, and as a wealthy commercial city, it excited the envy of its neighboring nations.

Finally the hour of our departure came and the patriarchal procession moved forward with its retinue. The procession was led by the Catholicos's magnificent landau carriage which was surrounded by about twenty mounted police-soldiers led by a Russian officer. The carriages of the Catholicos and his retinue of about twenty-five sped away from the crowd of Armenians in Alexandrapol in a cloud of dust. With the Gars River on our left, we moved between the fertile fields of blowing grass of the Shirag plain. We passed through the fields of grain, vast meadows, and cane fields; and often we passed thicketed hillocks and fields with brushwood. After two hours of moving at a fast pace we reached the wooden bridge of the Gars River, and we passed the site of Argina, the once famous Residence of the Catholicos of Khachatur, which is now in ruins. The Holy Patriarch was hosted for half an hour in a summerhouse here by a kind family from Yerevan, and then we continued our journey up the promontory of the Shirag plain. Our carriages moved fast, and as we approached Ani, our anticipation grew more intense, notwithstanding the thick clouds of dust and the burning sun which scorched us. We didn't care at all because we were filled with overflowing hearts that beat fast in longing and anguish and crazy haste to see Ani.

In the distance to the south we could see the white-haired Masis [Mt. Ararat], proud and imperious, which as Khorenatsi wrote "sprouted like a tree from the earth." The mountain rises like a colossal tree, or a monolithic tower of stone created by God, and it dominates the surroundings and the mountain chains around it. Everything is dwarfed next to Masis's awesome height (5,150 meters). Is not this mountain which rises on the heart of Armenia a silent monument to the ancient glory and sorrow of the Armenians?

In the distance to the east we could see the mountains of Gegharkunik with their snow-capped peaks and also the Bartogh mountains near Masis; and behind Ani we could see the mountains of Koghb, where the famous salt mines are, which Catholicos Yezr took as a bribe from the Greek emperor to assent to the Council of Chalcedon. And, in front of us stands Mt. Aragats with its four snow-capped peaks, and a little further on is Mt. Aray with its wooded northern slopes, which define the northern border of the vast Ararat plain. Finally, after a four-and-a-half hour trip, we began to descend that slope of the plain of Shirag from which the ruins of Ani appear as scattered black points. The closer we got, the larger those black points grew, and the first thing we saw were the great external walls and the colossal semicircular towers of Ani, built of polished stone.

We were whipped up by such overflowing emotions that we wanted to fly to kiss the earth of Ani and those holy relics made by the hands of our ancestors, whether a piece of a stone cross or a remnant of an old ruin. Finally we arrived at the huge outer ramparts, which in 1064 Alpaslan tried to destroy with his furious catapults. Indeed, it is impossible not to be affected by these sad monuments and their reminder of Ani's past glory. Ani's ruins do not leave visitors with the awe-inspiring impression of the ruins of Baalbek or the Acropolis of Athens; nor do they have the majestic appearance of the monumental columniated arches and beautiful labyrinths of the Acropolis. Ani, however, speaks more to the heart of the Armenian visitor than the eye, for these ruins still bear the imprint of the vandalism and barbarism of the Arabs, Seljuks, Persians, and Greeks. It seems as if those greedy enemies, who invaded from all directions, wanted to destroy Ani and expunge the past glory of this magnificent and prosperous capital of the Pakraduni kings.

Barely had we reached the great arcaded gate of Ani when Professor Marr and about forty of his workers, all with spades and pick-axes on their shoulders, walked toward us through a large crowd that had come from the area and from Alexandrapol. He greeted the Holy Patriarch and, after presenting him with salt and bread on a beautiful tray according to traditional custom, he delivered the following speech in Classical Armenian.

> Your Holiness, please accept with love the salt and bread of this place that I respectfully present to you. It is almost nine centuries since a patriarchal visit to Ani occurred, and it is with spontaneous and great excitement that I speak before these ruined and empty buildings.
>
> Welcome to one who was chosen by God's will from among the Armenian nation, confirmed by the Emperor of Russia, and who will soon be consecrated. May his gracious arrival—which is consoling, encouraging as well as exhorting—be good tidings for these forgotten monuments.
>
> Behold this site where it seems appropriate to remember the saying about restraint in regard to worldly grandeur, "Alas for this transitory glory."[79] In connection with the lives that have forever passed, there remains this superb manifestation of their spirit of building, all of which is brought into the light through these exca-

---

79. Translator: Quotation from Movses Khorenatsi, *History of the Armenians* 2.13.

vations. Furthermore, these ruins that are now being revived by scientific knowledge will become precious gems of truth in the larger
wellspring of knowledge, and they will also fill the intellectual storehouse of your spiritual children, the descendants of Hayk.

Of [all] this I am certainly not a master, but I can confirm and
witness it. The profound wisdom of this place does not need a translator or interpreter. The rocks of Ani and their many ornaments,
many writings and many languages,[80] which you will soon see with
your eyes and feel with your hands, will teach us more deeply than
anyone among us. And resulting from the death of the material Ani,
there is [now] the celestial Ani, the picturesque Ani, and the scientific Ani. And because you were zealous to arrive here, sometimes
passing through difficulties in order to reach your capital, so this
will strengthen our hope that Ani will exist not only for the scholars but will also live again for the world.

And truly may the sun shine in abundance and may this new
and sublime cause of hope be glorified, for which I am thankful to
Your Holiness from the bottom of my heart. Welcome be your
arrival.

Long live His Holiness.

The crowd of people repeated twice and thrice Professor
Marr's last words, and the high-flying outcry "Long live His
Holiness" reverberated through the arches of Ani's ramparts, and
through the towers and ruins, echoing out to the distant caves
and forests of Dzaghatzor. When you recall that the man who
gave this speech in Classical Armenian is half English and half
Georgian and has a Russian wife, it is easy to forgive whatever
grammatical errors he made. I am happy to reproduce the speech
of this eminent Armenologist in order to disclose his immense
erudition. After listening to Professor Marr with much emotion
as well as patience under the burning sun, His Holiness the
Patriarch responded:

80. Translator: Presumably referring to the great variety of epigraphic languages found at Ani.

Yes, respected professor, these ruins which stand silently here remind the Armenian people of its glorious past, the beautiful days, those times when the staff of Armenian life shined brightly. You, venerable professor, are worthy of thanks, for you open the door to knowledge for the present generation and by means of your excavations present an immense service to the Armenian Nation. Through your excavations, you reveal to the whole world the true picture of the magnificent past of a misfortunate and exiled people. Throughout my whole life I have longed to see this moment and am very happy that today I have witnessed it. Please accept my thanks, noble Professor.

Then His Holiness the Catholicos and his retinue with their carriages entered the verdant main gate of the ramparts to find a red banner with the following words: "Welcome, Your Holiness Catholicos Matteos II." After an exhausting five-hour trip under the burning sun in dusty carriages, we descended to the royal gate at the southern side of Ani's cathedral.

Then, His Holiness the Catholicos of All Armenians, entered the Cathedral with his followers and a body of bishops, *vardapets*, and married priests from the surrounding villages as a dense crowd of pilgrims sang in harmony the soul-stirring hymn *"Urakh ler, Surb ekeghetsi* [Rejoice, O Holy Church]."

Oh, the scene was so moving and unprecedented. After nine long centuries, this was the first time that a Catholicos of All Armenians with an official patriarchal retinue visited Ani in a solemn fashion. Truly, since its destruction, Ani had not seen such a glorious day. On this occasion Ani took on the animation of its royal days, and among this crowd great excitement prevailed inside the ramparts and around the monastery.

The city of Ani had not seen such a great crowd since its destruction, as a multitude of Armenian pilgrims, group by group, came there from the surrounding cities and villages in order to see the famous ruins of their ancestors and their newly elected, beloved patriarch.

Ani's cathedral was too small for the great crowd. When the lofty pillars and triumphant arches of the cathedral resounded from the loud shrill voices of the hymn that was sung, at that moment, many wept, as they recalled the royal consecration of the Pakraduni kings Ashot the Merciful, Kakig I, and their successors in this Cathedral in the presence of the Patriarch of All Armenians, feudal lords, princes, and the crowd of people. It is difficult to see all this and not be moved, even though we must recall that every stone cross is irrigated with the blood and tears of the Armenians, and that however inglorious each ruin may be, and in collapse, it has an old story of its glory.

Then we exited the cathedral, and His Holiness the Patriarch went to rest in the monastery in Professor Marr's room, the best room and one that was prepared especially for him. After a two-hour repose and a meal, the Holy Patriarch with his retinue emerged to tour the ruins. Professor Marr led the group, and I took notes from his explanations in my travelogue, and as the architect Toros Toramanian was also with us, I was able to get his detailed scholarly explanations.

After indefatigably wandering through Ani's ruins and the Marr Museum for four hours we returned exhausted to take supper in the monastery and go to sleep. Despite our fatigue, we found it impossible to sleep because the pilgrims who had come were now assembled around the monastery or in nearby tents, and were eating and drinking and playing the *parkapzuk*[81] and *sring*[82] and made such a commotion it was difficult to even nap. It was then that many of us began to recall the events of our great journey, beginning with the Peterhof Palace of the tsars in Petersburg to the ruins of Ani. And being in these ruins, we were prompted to envision the faces of Armenian kings, princes, and military commanders, and history took form before our eyes. Several hours after midnight when the noisy tumult of the *sring*, *parkapzuk*, and village dances died down, the deadness of night came over the ancient ruins of Ani. Instead of the songs of Goghtn,[83] all we could hear were the occasional cries of owls.

---

81. Translator: A type of bagpipe.

82. Translator: A type of shepherd's flute.

83. Translator: a distinctive Armenian form of folk poetry inspired by pre-Christian traditions, as preserved in Movses Khorenatsi.

Before long, the sun's golden disk rose from the broad sides of
sweet Aragats. We left our pallets and, restored by several hours of
sleep, we rushed to breakfast. We continued our investigation of the
ruins, listening to Professor Marr and Toramanian. We came again
to the Cathedral. In front of its southern royal door the Holy Catholicos and his retinue were photographed, as is seen in the image
[in this volume]. Also at the request of Professor Marr, the Holy
Patriarch was photographed in the museum near the statue of
King Kakig I in such a position that you might think the king and
the Catholicos were speaking to each other.

(I feel it is unnecessary to recall the descriptions of all the ruins
that we visited because I have already noted them in detail in my
third chapter "Description of the Ruins of Ani.")

It is already noon. After eating a light meal, we prepare to return
from Ani toward Alexandrapol. The pilgrims assemble near the carriage of the Holy Catholicos. His Holiness blesses the people with
a patriarchal benediction. The procession begins to move. Suddenly
it passes in front of a famous Armenian minstrel named Kevork.
Several strings of a *chungur*[84] vibrate under the excited minstrel's
plectrum. The Catholicos is very moved, as we all become deeply
moved, especially when the minstrel asks us, on behalf of the ruins,
why we are departing, leaving them in oblivion and solitude.

Upon the command of the Russian officer, the police-soldiers
move forward. The carriages of the Holy Patriarch and all the members of the retinue follow amidst the discordant "long lives." When
we emerge from the external great gate of the walls we cast a final
glance behind us toward the sacred ruins of Ani which gradually
disappear from our sight. And, a quarter of an hour later we encounter the ruins of the Church of the Shepherd and then travel toward
Ghoshavank, where, after resting a little, we visit and observe all
the parts of this famous monastery, its pillared antechambers and
its meeting hall for the feudal lords. Then we descend with the village priest to a nearby valley where Ashod the Merciful's grave is

---

84. Translator: Also *chongur, chonguri,* or *choghur*—a stringed instrument
used in the Caucasus.

located. After kissing his grave, we again sit in our carriages and set off toward Argina, where we find a sumptuous feast. Here we rest for a good while and are invigorated. Then we continue our voyage toward Alexandrapol, where we encounter a majority of the people of the city who have come to greet us—in over a hundred carriages, on horses, and on foot.

The clouds of thick dust are overwhelming us. Carriages and horses strike one another; we can't see each other. Some carriages topple over in this chaos and confusion—all in honor of the Holy Patriarch. Finally, we reach the new and magnificent prelacy building of Alexandrapol where we had been received on our first visit. After baths and rest, we participated in an extravagant feast which the city of Alexandrapol organized in honor of the Holy Catholicos.

It was already dawn and silence reigned everywhere as we made our preparations for departure. The magnificent patriarchal train was ready. We moved in a solemn procession to the station. Again chaos, again confusion, and finally, amidst the high-flying yells of "long live" and "go in peace" issuing from the people, the train moves forward . . . toward Holy Etchmiadzin, taking with us the sweet and unforgettable memories which will remain ineffaceable for life.

ODE TO THE CITY OF ANI[85]
The city of Ani sits, it cries,
There is no one saying do not cry, do not cry;
You say it is little, leave it, let it remain crying,
Akh, when will I hear don't cry, don't cry?
    I burn and grow scorched with pain,
    I do not have one faithful person
    Who comes glowing with compassion
    No one says no, don't cry, don't cry.

---

85. Translator: This poem is thought to date from the nineteenth century, and has been attributed to Alexander Araratian. See http://www.virtualani .org/ephemera/anipoem1.htm (accessed 24 September 2017); and Tadevos Hakobyan, *Anii patmutiwn* [The History of Ani], vol. 2 (Yerevan: Yerevan State University Press, 1982), 389–390.

Exhortation

Akh, Armenian lad, have pity on me,
See how your Ani is,
It is enough, that I cry and you do not commiserate,
Is it not that your Ani is a pity?

 My days passed with sighs and groans,
 My eyes grew blind from crying;
 I was fated to remain an orphan,
 My fate never forgot me

I have lost kings,
Blind owls assembled around my head
And always sing, "Ani is gone,
Ani, without its master, was ruined."

 I am Ani very populous,
 I am left bitter ruins;
 My weeping, my lamentation and cry,
 Is like that of abandoned orphans.

At one time I was unequalled,
The eastern city of the Armenians;
I have been demolished to the ground,
Sitting I cry alone.

 You came and saw, you turn about and leave,
 Crying you say, "stay well."
 For the love of God, do not forget
 When you approach Mt. Masis . . .[86]

Say to my brave Ararat,
"*Your poor Ani sits and cries*";
It asks when will you give good news . . .
That "You have cried enough, my Ani . . ."

I have closed with this old folk song so that we might remember
that Ani has always been close to the heart of the Armenian people,
and its destruction has been always lamented.

---

86. Translator: Ararat.

Acknowledgments

My gratitude to Doris Varjabedian Cross for her editing and to Liz Bodian for her editing and assistance throughout; to Christina Maranci for her generosity in coming to the rescue many times with her linguistic and scholarly expertise, and to Mr. Harutiun Maranci for his linguistic expertise; to Rachel Goshgarian for being an exceptional guide on my first trip to Ani; to Hourig Sahagian for the generous gift of an inscribed first edition of Krikor Balakian's *Ruins of Ani*, which provided a unique connection to the journey.

Much gratitude to the Research Council at Colgate University for support at crucial junctures of this project, including travel to Ani in 2014 and 2015. And to Jim and Janet Balakian and the Balakian Foundation for support at crucial moments in the translation process. Aram Arkun's work as translator and scholar has been invaluable and exemplary. I'm grateful to Lisa Banning, my editor at Rutgers University Press, for her good work throughout.

Glossary

Certain proper nouns are given in Eastern/Classical spellings and in Western Armenian in parentheses.

Akhurian River. River that runs through the South Caucasus, originating in Armenia and flowing from Lake Arpi, along the border with Turkey, forming part of the geographic border between the two states. Today the river flows along a border that has been closed by Turkey.

Alexandrapol (Gyumri). Second-largest city in Armenia and the bureaucratic center of Shirak Province. In the nineteenth century it was known as Alexandropol and was one of the largest cities of Russian-ruled Armenia. It was renamed Leninakan during the Soviet period.

Alpaslan (1029–1072) *(Alp Arslan, Muhammad bin Davud Chaghri).* The second sultan of the Seljuk Empire. He greatly expanded Seljuk territory and consolidated power, and his victory over the Byzantines at Manzikert (1071) ushered in the Turkish settlement of Anatolia. Because of his military prowess he was named *Alpaslan*, "Heroic Lion" in Turkish.

Amira. A member of a wealthy class of Armenian nobility, mostly in Constantinople. The *amiras* were often put in charge of Armenian matters in the Ottoman Empire, especially before the 1860 Armenian National Constitution, and they were often powerful financiers who managed the finances of the Turkish elite.

Ashot (Ashod) I (c. 820–890). Armenian king of the Bagratuni (Pakraduni) dynasty who ruled during the beginning of what is sometimes called Armenia's second golden age (862–977). He was known as Ashot the Great and was the son of Smbat VIII the Confessor.

Bagratuni (Pakraduni) dynasty. The Bagratuni family were dominant rulers of various regions of medieval Armenia, including Syunik, Van, Taron, and Tayk.

Byzantine emperors. Some who were Armenian included Heraclius (c. 575–641), Mizizios (668–669), Artavazdos (741–732), and Leo the Armenian (775–820).

Catholicos. The head of all the Armenian churches, a rank analogous to Pope.

Charmaghan (Chormaqan Noyan) (died c. 1241). One of the most famous generals of the Mongol Empire under Genghis Khan and Ogedei Khan.

Etchmiadzin. The center of the Armenian Apostolic Church. Inhabited since the third millennium B.C., it was the home of the Mother Cathedral and the seat of the Church in the fourth century. While the location of the Catholicate shifted in subsequent centuries, it returned to Etchmiadzin from Sis in Cilicia in 1441. Today it is the fourth-largest city in Armenia and is located just 11 miles west of the capital Yerevan.

Fetvadjian, Arshag (1866–1947). Artist and designer. He is best known for his watercolor paintings of the architectural monuments of Ani, and for designing the currency and postage stamps of the first Republic of Armenia (1918–1920).

Gagik I (Kakig). King of Armenia between 989 and c. 1017/20, under whom Bagratid Armenia reached its height.

Gagik II (Kakig II) (c. 1025–1079). The king of Ani and the last Armenian king of the Bagratuni dynasty. He was a juvenile at the time he was enthroned and ruled for a brief period (1042–1045) before the Pakraduni dynasty collapsed.

Genghis Khan (born *Temüjin*) (1162–1227). The Great Khan and founder of the Mongol Empire, which became the largest contiguous empire in history after his death. He came to power by uniting many of the nomadic tribes of Northeast Asia.

Hayk the Great (Hayk Nahapet Hayk). The legendary patriarch and founder of the Armenian nation. His story is told in the *History of Armenia* attributed to the Armenian historian Movses Khorenatsi (410–490).

Horomos Monastery (Ghoshavank). Abandoned and ruined medieval Armenian monastic complex about 5 kilometers northeast of the ruins of Ani. Horomos was founded by a group of Armenian monks around 931–936, during the reign of King Abas I Pakraduni (r. c. 929–953). It was once of the most significant religious and cultural centers in the Christian East. Some time after 1965, the Monastery of Horomos was partly destroyed, most likely as part of the Turkish government's policy of cultural genocide.

Hovhannes-Smbat III. Bagratid king (1020–1040). He succeeded his father Gagik I of Ani (989–1020).

Katramide (Gadranite). The first queen of the Bagratid kingdom as wife of the first Bagratuni king, Ashot the Great (885–890).

Khatchkar (khachkar). An Armenian carved stone cross. The crosses bear intricate vine and rosette motifs, as well as pagan and Christian iconography. The khatchkar is a dominant Armenian folk art prevalent in the landscape.

Khorenatsi (Horenatsi), Movses (c. A.D. 410–490s). Prominent Armenian historian and writer, author of the *History of Armenia,* the first attempt at a universal history of Armenia.

Lynch, H.F.B. (Henry Finnis Blosse Lynch, 1862–1913). British traveler, businessman, and Liberal Member of Parliament. His two-volume book, *Armenia: Travels and Studies* (1901) is a singular work bringing together history, politics, archaeology, and travel writing.

Marr, Nicholas (Nikolai) (1865–1934). Georgia-born historian and linguist who gained a reputation as a scholar of the Caucasus during the 1910s before embarking on his "Japhetic theory" on the origin of language. Marr was sent with a small team to undertake the first proper excavations at the Armenian "lost" city of Ani during the summer of 1892. Marr did extraordinary work at Ani overseeing teams of archaeologists through more than two decades of digs.

Matteos Izmerlian II (1845–1910). The Catholicos of All Armenians of the Armenian Apostolic Church at the Mother See of Holy Etchmiadzin 1908–1910. He succeeded Mkrtich I Khrimian, who was Catholicos from 1892 to 1907.

Nakharar. The highest hereditary title given to families and houses of ancient and medieval Armenian nobility.

Primate. Title of high-ranking esteem given to some archbishops by the diocesan headquarters of the church.

Sanahin. Church and monastery founded in the tenth century in the Lori Province is a dramatic complex with an extraordinary array of *khachkars* in the northern mountains of Armenia.

Seljuks. Sunni Muslim Turkic tribes originating from the Qiniq branch of Oghuz Turks. In the eleventh and twelfth centuries, the Seljuk Empire controlled areas that spanned from the Hindu Kush to western Anatolia and from Central Asia to the Persian Gulf. With the Battle of Manzikert, they took control of eastern Anatolia and Armenia.

Shirak (Shirag) plain. Located in the Armenian highlands in the northwest part of Armenia today, and stretching from the left bank of the Akhurian River at the west, to the Pambak Mountains at the east. The plain is dominated by the Shirak mountains from the north.

Smbat I (850–912/14). The second king of the medieval Kingdom of Armenia of the Bagratuni dynasty, and son of Ashot I. He is the father of Ashot II (known as Ashot Yerkat) and Abas I.

Smbat II. Part of the Bagratuni line of kings, reigned as king of Armenia from 977 to 989. He was the son of Ashot III, whom he succeeded.

Tamerlane (1336–1405). A Turco-Mongol conqueror. As the founder of the Timurid Empire in Persia and Central Asia he became the first ruler in the Timurid dynasty. His troops were known for pillaging, raping, and massacring the many nations and peoples they ran over as they conquered large parts of the Eurasian steppes.

Toramanian, Toros (1864–1934). A prominent architect and architectural historian. He is considered "the father of Armenian architectural historiography."

Trdat III (Drtad III). King of Arsacid Armenia (287–330), and also known as Trdat the Great. In 301 he proclaimed Christianity as the state religion of Armenia, making the Armenian kingdom the first state to officially adopt Christianity.

Index

Page references with an f indicate illustrations.

About the Authors

KRIKOR BALAKIAN, 1876–1934, was one of the leading Armenian intellectuals of his generation. Educated at the Armenian Sanassarian Academy and Armash Seminary in Ottoman Turkey, and at Mittweida University and University of Berlin in Germany, he was one of the 250 cultural leaders arrested on April 24 by the Turkish government at the outset of the Armenian Genocide. He was imprisoned in Çhankiri and then survived nearly four years in the killing fields and shortly thereafter wrote a two-volume survivor memoir *Armenian Golgotha*. He was a member of the Armenian delegation to the Paris Peace Conference in 1919, and afterward became the pastor of the Armenian Church in Manchester, England, until the mid-1920s after which he was made Bishop of the Armenian Church of south France. He notes in his writings that he had written several other book manuscripts, which have subsequently disappeared. He died in Marseilles in 1934.

PETER BALAKIAN is the author of many books, including *Ozone Journal*, which won the 2016 Pulitzer Prize for poetry, *Black Dog of Fate*, winner of the PEN/Albrand Award for memoir, and *The Burning Tigris: The Armenian Genocide and America's Response*, winner of the Raphael Lemkin Prize. He is co-translator of Grigoris Balakian's *Armenian Golgotha: A Memoir of the Armenian Genocide*. He is Donald M. and Constance H. Rebar Professor of the Humanities in the department of English at Colgate University.

ARAM ARKUN is the executive director of the Tekeyan Cultural Association and an assistant editor at the *Armenian Mirror-Spectator*.